# MAGICALLY
# BLACK
## AND OTHER
# ESSAYS

---

# JERALD
# WALKER

# MAGICALLY BLACK

# AND OTHER

# ESSAYS

---

# JERALD WALKER

AMISTAD

*An Imprint of HarperCollinsPublishers*

MAGICALLY BLACK AND OTHER ESSAYS. Copyright © 2024 by Jerald Walker. All rights reserved. Printed in the United States of America. No part of this book may be used or reproduced in any manner whatsoever without written permission except in the case of brief quotations embodied in critical articles and reviews. For information, address HarperCollins Publishers, 195 Broadway, New York, NY 10007.

HarperCollins books may be purchased for educational, business, or sales promotional use. For information, please email the Special Markets Department at SPsales@harpercollins.com.

FIRST EDITION

*Designed by Janet Evans-Scanlon*
*Image on title page and chapter-opening pages © photodeedooo*
*/stock.adobe.com*

Library of Congress Cataloging-in-Publication Data

Names: Walker, Jerald, author.
Title: Magically Black and other essays / Jerald Walker.
Description: First edition. | New York, NY : Amistad, 2024.
Identifiers: LCCN 2024003410 (print) | LCCN 2024003411 (ebook)
  | ISBN 9780063161078 (hardcover) | ISBN 9780063161047
  (trade paperback) | ISBN 9780063161061 (ebook)
Subjects: LCSH: Walker, Jerald. | African Americans—
  Massachusetts—Biography. | African Americans—Race
  identity—History. | Racism—United States—History. | United
  States—Race relations—History.
Classification: LCC F71.22.W35 A3 2024 (print) | LCC F71.22.W35
  (ebook) | DDC 305.896/073--dc23/eng/20240410
LC record available at https://lccn.loc.gov/2024003410
LC ebook record available at https://lccn.loc.gov/2024003411

24 25 26 27 28 LBC 5 4 3 2 1

For Brenda, *always*.

*Like most modern people, I don't believe in prophecy or magic and then spend half my time practicing it.*

—JOHN STEINBECK,
*The Winter of Our Discontent*

# CONTENTS

## PROLOGUE
## The Curse

A marketer-turned-cult-leader fond of sending tweets, known in his day as newsletters. He sent several a month, increasing the frequency when soliciting money or responding to his critics and bad press. Sometimes for no apparent reason, but usually out of rage, he capitalized words. And by the time of his death in 1986, at the age of ninety-three, he'd had much to rage about, having been credibly accused of profiteering, racism, white supremacy, incest, embezzlement, tax evasion, narcissism, and compulsive lying, but not of treason, fascism, sedition, espionage, or obstruction of justice, so any comparisons of Herbert W. Armstrong to Donald J. Trump only go so far. They do, however, go far enough to include having among their converts some seriously misguided Black folk, including, in Armstrong's case, my parents.

Longtime fans of his television and radio religious broadcasts, my parents joined Armstrong's cult in 1957. The cult was named the Radio Church of God, and my parents believed it was a legitimate church and that Armstrong was the Messiah. Armstrong possibly believed he was the Messiah too, handpicked by God not only to deliver the Word, but to deliver it in style with private jets and limousines. In order to be taken seriously, after all, as God's spokesperson, he had to exude success, much like Trump would exude on *The Apprentice*.

I *loved The Apprentice*. I *loved* Trump. I couldn't get enough of watching him evaluate the contestants before pointing at one and saying *You're fired!* For laughs I bought a little button that when pressed said *You're fired!* in Trump's voice, and whenever my sons did something silly or my wife disagreed with me, I would point the little button at them and press it. After a while it turned up missing, so I bought another one, which soon went missing too. But, whatever. The phrase had gotten old and, besides, Trump had become a birther, so I quit watching the show.

And then he left the show to run for president and became must-watch TV again. I found him highly entertaining, a mixture of Don Rickles, Andrew Dice Clay, and David Duke, his outrageous comments often leaving me in stitches. He became less entertaining, though, when racists started coming out of the woodwork in support of him, including the actual David Duke. There was no entertainment left to be had after Confederate flags began appearing at his rallies. But I continued to watch them just to see how bad things could get, until I got triggered one evening when the camera panned the crowd and hovered on a young man and woman who, should the reason for their presence be unclear, wore T-shirts that read "Blacks for Trump." At least, I thought, my parents never stooped to wearing "Blacks for Armstrong" apparel.

Maybe they would have, though, had Armstrong not required local church services to be racially segregated. The only integrated services occurred during a few of the seven Holy Days, such as the weeklong Feast of Tabernacles that was observed in the form of regional conventions located all around the country—indeed, certainly after membership peaked at a quarter million in the 1970s, located all around the world. Armstrong would make a brief appearance at as many of these locations as possible, a validation of his jets and limousines and of the 30 percent tithing required of each household.

That 30 percent was hard on a poor, seven-child household like mine. The cost to attend the Feast of Tabernacles made it harder still, but the debt my parents incurred to do so, they felt, was well worth it, given the opportunity to see Armstrong in person. But I can recall seeing him in person only once, when I was seven or eight. My memory of the occasion, tainted by time's passage and Trump's ubiquity, places Armstrong at a podium, where he pauses delivering a typically terrifying sermon to scan the sea of nearly all white worshippers, at last locating a Black one before thrusting a finger in his direction and exclaiming, "Look at my Canaanite!"

"Canaanites," people versed in the Book of Genesis will know, were born of a mistake made by Noah. One night, the story goes, Noah consumed too much wine and decided to be naked for a while, which turned out to be all night because he fell asleep while still disrobed. His son Ham discovered him in this state and told his two brothers. Ham's two brothers, walking backward toward their father so as not to commit the unpardonable offense of gazing upon a parent's nakedness, covered Noah with a blanket. When Noah learned his nakedness had in fact been gazed upon by Ham, he cursed Ham's son, Canaan, proclaiming, "a servant of servants shall he be to his brothers." Armstrong interpreted this to mean that Canaan and his descendants were destined to attend to the needs of the Holy Race, i.e., white people, be it as slaves in cotton fields or cashiers at Macy's. To distinguish Canaanites from other races, God "marked" them with darker skin. Thus, the Negro.

Thus, too, I deduced, a lesson in imprudence. Had Noah exposed himself while sober, or even only mildly inebriated, it is unlikely he would have fallen into a deep slumber. He would have dozed off, to be sure, being a male of a certain age (nearly six hundred years old), but doubtlessly within arm's reach of his toga, thereby having time to cover himself upon being awakened by the sound of approaching sandals. Waking, instead, to the sound of his children's giggles, and with a blanket heaped upon his loins, Noah was left to stew in anger, the very trait, Armstrong maintained, that primarily characterized Black people.

My parents were not among the Black people who stewed in anger, but I wish they had been. Maybe then they would not have joined Armstrong's church, thereby sparing me, in 1964, from being born into it.

Not that I minded at first. To the contrary, I was grateful, as church members would soon be taken to the Place of Safety while everyone else went through some things. Armstrong had prophesied that at the start of the Great Tribulation in 1972, God would unleash demons, earthquakes, hail, brimstone, famine, droughts, and locusts to reveal his glory and to prove he was not bluffing about ending the world in 1975. He was bluffing, though; 1972 and 1975 came and went without incident. For a while there, 1978 looked promising for some terrible events, but they did not pan out either. Most church members were confused by this, until 1979, when Mike Wallace of *60 Minutes* did an exposé on the Radio Church of God—now renamed the Worldwide Church of God—revealing it to be a mixture of quackery, corruption, and greed. Armstrong was not the Messiah. No terribleness would be unleashed while we were in the Place of Safety. The world's end was not imminent. Moreover, whites were not the Holy Race, and Blacks were not destined to serve them.

This was good to know. But it would have been better to have known it sooner, because in 1979, I was fifteen and the damage was done. Along with accepting the myth of white supremacy, I had been denied meaningful exposure to Black traditions and culture. The Worldwide Church of God, for example, followed strict Levitical dietary laws that forbade its members from eating "unclean" foods, which meant no chitlins, pork ribs and neck bones, or fried catfish. We were discouraged from listening to music with profane lyrics or sexual innuendo or that implored us to make it funky, thereby eliminating much of blues and R&B and certainly Lucille Bogan, Chuck Willis, and James Brown. Our Afros were not supposed to be spectacular like Sly Stone's or Angela Davis's, and our speech had to be proper, which is to say free of slang and excessively rhythmic cadences. And in response to a racist society, we could not march, sit in, fist-raise, riot, or even curse white folk, since a racist society, Armstrong preached, was also God's plan.

But we could be and were full of ourselves. That was impossible to avoid considering the Kingdom of Heaven would admit only exceptional Blacks, the best of the very best, and these were the Blacks, Armstrong led us to believe, whom God had called. When you have been identified by God as exceptional and are estranged from Black traditions and culture, it is a small leap to conclude that you are not really Black at all. Some church members took that leap—figuratively, of course, lest they be accused of catching the Holy Ghost, which was forbidden too.

I had been close to taking that leap by the time I was thirteen, which was why I had not been swept up by all the hype for the miniseries *Roots*. When my family gathered in the living room to watch the first episode in January 1977, my mother and I excused ourselves and went to the kitchen to play Scrabble. She felt the series would be too painful to endure, whereas I, tentatively self-identifying as an "Israelite," had decided the story of Black enslavement had little to do with me. And yet, only minutes into the episode's start, I was lured back to the living room by the sound of beating drums, as if in subconscious response to the ancestors' call. I stared transfixed at the television for a long time before easing into a chair, as I would two years later with the *60 Minutes* exposé, when much of what I believed about myself, and race, would come undone.

Some therapy at that point would have been helpful. I also could have benefited from the mentorship of a few positive Black role models. Rather, I managed my trauma with various legal and illegal substances and sought to emulate men who, like Armstrong, were on the take. In this way I unleashed my very own personal Great Tribulation, which lasted, unlike the one Armstrong had prophesied, ten years instead of three.

It is no wonder, then, in light of my childhood, that I was initially drawn to Trump—this ultra-confident, charismatic, rich white man who claimed to be perfect and all-knowing— before I came to despise him. It is no wonder, either, that the first time I saw the Blacks for Trump, I was triggered.

*Why the hell*, I wanted to know, were they *for* him? Had they merely transferred their fandom of *The Apprentice* to MAGA? Had they convinced themselves Trump was the Messiah? Were they insufficiently angry? Did they think that supporting a white supremacist made them exceptional Blacks, the best of the very best? Or maybe they were former members of Armstrong's cult, still believing Blacks to be Canaan's cursed descendants. I hoped not. That story's preposterous.

The true story, people versed in *Roots* will know, goes more like this: A man paced anxiously outside his hut, inside of which his wife was in labor. Now and then, her distressed cries pierced the air until, suddenly, following a brief silence, there was a baby's wail. The man smiled with relief after a doula emerged from the hut to summon him inside to meet his firstborn, a son. Eight days later, as was the naming custom, the father carried his son from the hut into the dark of night and laid him upon the ground. He removed the child's blanket, exposing his nakedness. "Kunta Kinte," he said, lifting the child up to the heavens, up to God. "Behold: the only thing greater than yourself."

Thus, the Negro.

Thus, me.

# MAGICALLY BLACK

A stack of syllabi . . . thirty undergrads . . . two transparent cups, one containing coffee, the other milk . . . a dropper . . .

And overhead, a wall clock indicating the fall 2003 semester has begun . . .

. . . I rise from my desk and introduce myself as "Dr. J," a nod to my all-time favorite basketball player and the impostor syndrome being called this nickname lessens. *The classroom is my court*, I tell myself, *and I've got game*, but in reality I have only been teaching for a year and I am not very confident about what I am doing, other than my ability to turn people Black.

I lift the cup of milk. "Does anyone know what this is?"

The student nearest me excitedly waves her hand, as if I have asked the question for which she has long prepared. I call on her.

"Milk!" she erupts.

"Very good."

She opens her notepad and writes, I presume, "Milk."

I lift the other cup, but this time before I can ask the

question several hands rise, a correct answer having inspired confidence, and some cockiness too; a few students slouch and smirk, even as one of them mumbles, "Coffee."

"Excellent." After replacing both cups, I pick up the dropper. I fill it with coffee, hold it a foot above the milk, release a drop, and then raise the milk high and pan it for all to see, like David Copperfield with the changed card. "Now what is it?"

"Milk," someone answers, "*with* coffee."

"Incorrect," I say.

A clever student remarks, "Coffee *with milk*?"

"Wrong again."

Someone jokes *café au lait*, which leads to a comical listing of half the Starbucks menu before I settle everyone down: "What was once milk," I tell them, "is now . . . coffee."

The first response is instant, fake-coughed into a palm from the back of the room: "*Bullshit.*"

I do not dispute this. Nor do I object to the term. I am in small-town Massachusetts, teaching mostly first-generation college students, the children of parents who work with their hands and not a few of whom, I suspect, settle disputes with them too. The campus atmosphere is distinctly blue-collar, the coeds tough but not mean, cynical but not nihilistic, aggressive but not rude, much like me, I'd like to think, when on my best behavior.

"*Total* bullshit," I say. "And yet this is the rule by which race in this country has for centuries been determined: *one* drop of Black blood subsumes all others. But the thing about rules is that they often originate not from logic but power. In other words, whoever is in charge gets to make them. I, for instance, being in charge of this class, have made several rules you must follow, such as addressing me, at *all* times, as 'Dr. J.'" I pause to move in front of my desk, as advised by a book I am reading on how to be an effective teacher. It is effective, the book says, to move in front of your desk when you are about to light a bomb. "My most *important* rule, however, is that you accept this premise: at the moment I added that drop of coffee to the milk, a drop of Black blood was added to you."

A sloucher to my left bolts upright, which reminds me that last year, the first time I taught this course, I had the same reaction from another student, who happened to be my only Black one, exactly one more than I have now. When I explained that for the duration of the semester everyone had to agree to be Black, he assured me he already was. And then his offended expression slowly gave way to a smile, as it maybe dawned on him that taking the course would be the same as having the answers in advance of an exam.

This sloucher does not smile. To the contrary, he frowns as he asks, "Do you mean, like, we have to wear blackface?"

"Please don't," I say.

"Professor?"

I turn to the student who just spoke and remind her of how I must be addressed.

"Sorry, *Dr. J*," she says, rolling her eyes. "Um, we won't have to rap, will we? Because I'm no good at that."

She *is* smiling, so I cannot tell if she is serious, but I am fairly certain the young man is who offers to teach her. He's wearing a Tupac T-shirt and a thick gold necklace. I say rapping's optional.

Another student folds his arms over his chest before speaking. "No offense, Dr. J, but I don't really *want* to be Black."

"You are not alone," I tell him.

"*I* do," someone says. It is the student who wrote "Milk" on her notepad. Next to "Milk," I can see, she has added, "Magically Black."

"And you," I say, "are not alone either."

———

Hannah is a house slave who has been given the task of waiting on her master's new bride. The first thing Hannah notices about the bride is her nervous, distressed state, and eventually, once the two women have become close, the bride confides in Hannah the reason: she is Black, which is to say, in the vernacular of the class, there is a drop of coffee in her milk. Moreover, someone else knows it and is threatening to expose her; pay up, or be responsible for the ruin of the man she loves, to say nothing of being enslaved, if not executed. Hannah, whose complexion, like her mistress's, bears no evidence of her African heritage, suggests they flee. These events are unfolding in the first book on the reading list, *The Bondwoman's Narrative*, by Hannah Crafts. "Hannah Crafts" is the pseudonym of the former slave who wrote it.

The events are also unfolding, hopefully, with my course description still fresh in the students' minds:

*Finding yourself suddenly Black and wishing to sur-*
*vive (and ultimately to thrive) in a society that often*
*does not value its Black citizens, there are some impor-*
*tant things you will need to know. Fortunately for*
*you, your ancestors are among the world's preeminent*
*survivors, and they can teach you very much. They*
*have been teaching Blacks how to survive for four*
*hundred years now, and so their methods are proven.*
*To receive this wisdom, all you have to do is to study*
*the survival strategies recorded over the years in what*
*is collectively known as the African American Novel.*

"What survival strategy," I ask at the start of our first discussion, "does Hannah find useful as she embarks upon such
a dangerous mission?"

Someone answers, "Having white-looking skin."

"Having white-looking skin," I say, "is not exactly a strategy. Think in terms of the whole race, something *all* Blacks,
regardless of complexion, could adopt."

"Some *guns*," someone else says. He grins at the young
man next to him.

The young man next to him grins back. *"Hells yeah!"* he
agrees. "Kill *all* them honkies!"

According to my book on effective teaching, I am supposed to respond thoughtfully to all student comments rather
than laugh or call them dumb. This is not easy. It helps when
I say, "Okay, let's think about this," because that gives me a
little extra time to keep it together. I say this now, and then,
because I still need more time, I stroke my chin while pacing

the room. When I feel composed enough to maintain a straight face, I note the unlikelihood of Hannah having had access to guns, and that, even if such was not the case, she probably would not have known how to use them. "Also," I add, "based on what we know of her so far, in terms of her personality and values, would it ever cross her mind to say, or even to think, 'Kill all them honkies'?"

"I'm just talking about what *I* would do, you know, as a *brother*."

"For the moment," I say, "talk about Hannah. How would you describe her as a person? Anyone?"

A student raises her hand and offers, "Nice?"

"Yes! And one could say her niceness derives from what?" Silence.

I rephrase the question: "What are her values based on?"

"Her house-slavery?"

"Her hope for freedom?"

"Her white-looking skin?"

"Her coffee?"

"Her *milk*!"

"Okay, let's think about this." I direct the class to a key passage and read it aloud: "'I had much to make me miserable and discontented. The life of a slave is at best not a pleasant one, but I had formed a resolution to always look on the bright side of things. . . . I can never be great, nor rich; I cannot hold an elevated position in society, but I can do my duty, and be kind in the sure and certain hope of an external reward." Pay attention, I tell the students, to the fact that Hannah makes references to God in every chapter, and pretty much on every page. "Faith, optimism, *hope*," I stress, "broadly defined as the tenets of religion, were invaluable to her, as they were to many enslaved people, in their quest to endure their plight." This is important, the students recognize. Their first survival strategies. As they write them down, I wait for a counterargument, but it does not come.

It did last year. A student insisted that religion had historically been used to suppress the masses, to make them sheep in this life while they foolishly waited for salvation in the next. That raised some objections among the religious students, one of whom overcame her sheepishness to call him an asshole. This kind of exchange can be fruitful for a discussion-centered course such as mine, but it is problematic if the course is also text-centered and there are no examples of non-sheepish religious figures on the syllabus. I'd made an unforced error, akin in basketball to missing a layup or dribbling off my shoe. This time I have assigned *Black Thunder*.

*Black Thunder* is based on the true story of a Virginian slave revolt that occurred in 1800. Over one thousand captives intended to break into an arsenal, giving them access to enough weapons to kill every white person in Richmond. The hope was that once word of the uprising spread, enslaved people all across the South would rise up against their oppressors. It was a daring, ambitious plan, and it might have worked but for two misfortunes: a freak rainstorm at the designated hour that washed out the roads leading to the arsenal, and the betrayal by a slave whose loyalties were to his master rather than to his kin. Upon learning of the plot, the white community was horrified. It was also convinced that one of their own had concocted it, for no Negro mind, they believed, was capable of doing so. But a Negro's mind was and had. It belonged to an enslaved man named Gabriel Prosser.

Gabriel Prosser, in addition to being inspired by the ongoing Haitian slave revolt that began in 1791, believed that Negroes' right to be free was supported by the Bible, including this passage from Exodus 21: "He that stealeth a man and selleth him, or if he be found in his hand, he shall surely be put to death." That passage in particular excited the fictional Gabriel, and conceivably the real Gabriel as well, but while the real Gabriel could read, the fictional one was illiterate and had to rely on a fellow enslaved person, Mingo, to deliver the divine message to their recruits. "That the scripture," Gabriel would explain. "That's the *good* book what Mingo's reading out of." And when Mingo read words like "oppression" and "judgment" and "salvation," Gabriel emphasized them before driving the message home: "Y'all heard what he read," he said once. "God's aiming to give them in the hands of they enemies and all like of that. He say he just need a man to make up the hedge and stand in the gap. He's going to cut them down his own self. See?" All the enslaved nodded. They saw.

I hope my students see too. I am encouraged when they take notes as I explain how religion not only gave enslaved people faith, hope, and optimism, it offered confirmation of their will toward dignity and self-determination. "But religion did not," I add, "*give* them the courage to act on this will. That was *in them*, and, because it was *in them*, it is, as their descendants, *in you!*" This is a strong sentence. I rehearsed delivering it in the mirror many times, pointing at my reflection and imagining my students filling with pride as I had when I first thought of it, even if, for them, according to the reflections in their mirrors, the descendant part was not true. But while I am new to the classroom, I am not new to the ways of human nature; everyone likes the idea of having courageous ancestors. It is no surprise to me, then, that after the delivery of my strong sentence, some slouchers sit more upright, and some grumpy students smile, and one student, my rapper, silently moved his lips as I spoke, converting my words to the lyrics, I imagine, of some materializing song. If so, the song will be bittersweet. Upon the failure of Gabriel's plan, he, along with dozens of his followers, was hanged.

During his trial, the real Gabriel refused to take the stand. And he made no final statement as he awaited the gallows. Arna Bontemps, however, the author of the fictionalized account, took the liberty of dramatizing Gabriel's acceptance of his fate by having him say, after the hangman asked if he would like to speak, "Let the rope talk, suh. The rope, please you suh, let it talk."

"Why," I ask the class, "does Gabriel refuse to defend himself?"

There is a brief pause before a student speaks. "Humanity," she says, "is its own defense." All the students nod. They see. When students see, according to my teaching book, the instructor should respond with great enthusiasm: applause, for instance, or even a rousing cheer, as opposed to, say, hugs.

"You did not," my wife, Brenda, asks that evening, "hug your student?"

"Plural," I clarify.

"You hugged her more than once?"

"No. I hugged them all."

Brenda places her fork on her plate in order to concentrate on staring at me. She maintains her concentration for a long time, even after our three-year-old, Adrian, begins washing the table with his milk, and when, across from him in his high chair, Dorian, who's one, pitches his Cheerios to the floor. We are having dinner, though I believe it has just concluded, and Brenda and I are discussing how our classes went that day. She is a naturally gifted teacher and therefore does not consult a book on how to do it effectively, and she does not hug her students.

"I feared that hugging only one of them," I try to explain, "especially a female, would be seen as creepy."

"So you tried to eliminate the creep factor by multiplying it?" She shakes her head, inside of which, I am certain, is an image of me speaking to the director of human resources. This image is in my head too. In my version, I am attributing my mistake to the students so thoroughly getting it that I was thrown off my game. Rather than staring at me or shaking her head, however, the director of human resources says it sounds like I am balling up in there and no wonder my students call me Dr. J and maybe it's time for a raise, but when she asks for my plate the image vanishes and Brenda is at the sink, extending her hand. After I bring her my plate, she says, "I hope this doesn't land you in Human Resources."

"Maybe it will. Maybe it will and I'll end up getting a raise out of it."

She chuckles, despite herself. I'm glad the tension is broken. I attempt to build on the improved atmosphere by reiterating my unprecedented success.

"It's not unprecedented," she corrects me.

"It's not?"

"You told me something similar happened last year. Several students fist-pumped, you said, as you were going on about courage and bravery while jabbing everywhere."

"I don't *jab everywhere*. I point. Strategically. With precision and control."

"Maybe so when you're in class, but when you do it in the mirror, it looks kind of wild."

I have to work on my pointing. Luckily, I am not scheduled to do it again until near the end of the semester when I am lamenting a white female being murdered and set ablaze. Until then, the focus will be on Black females, only one of whom, the mother of the title character in Toni Morrison's *Sula*, our next novel, will end up in flames.

Ten-year-old Sula actually watches the flaming occur, having just glanced out her bedroom window when sparks of an open fire ignite her mother's dress. Curiously, as her mother is consumed by the fire, Sula does not scream or call for help. Her failure to act possibly stems from the sheer horror of the situation, and yet it is inconceivable she would have responded similarly if the victim had been her best friend, Nell. Nell and Sula, by this early point of the novel, are inseparable. And they are mutually protective; this is why Nell prefers that they avoid the part of town where white boys are prone to harass Black girls, and why Sula, preferring that they go where they please, one day brings a knife. As they approach the boys, the boys, true to custom, advance on them with nefarious intentions, stopping only after Sula produces her weapon and brings it to one of her fingers. After watching her finger's severed tip land at her feet, she looks up at the boys and posits a troubling question: "If that's what I'll do to myself, what you suppose I'll do to you?" The boys, supposing the answer, flee.

When my class discusses this scene, a student says, "Sula's a *badass*." This opinion is met with broad consensus. And when I say that her friendship with Nell is indicative of Black unity, such as we saw between Hannah and her mistress, and that, more to the point, Black unity as a survival strategy is especially meaningful to Black women, there is more consensus. Consensus, however, my teaching book cautions, is a desirable end but not always a desirable means because it precludes debate. To keep discussions lively, instructors must play devil's advocate. But screw the devil. The class is going well, so I decide to direct everyone to an especially pro-Black-female-unity passage and read it to them: "Because each had discovered years before they were neither white nor male, and that all freedom and triumph was forbidden to them, they had to set about creating something else to be. Their meeting was fortunate, for it let them use each other to grow. . . . They found in each other's eyes the intimacy they were looking for." On that note, the class period ends in perfect harmony, a stark contrast to how the next one begins.

"Sula's a *traitor*," one student says.

"No different," adds another, "than that slave who snitched on Gabriel."

"Okay," I say. "Let's think about this."

"There's *nothing* to think about, Dr. J!"

"She *slept* with Nell's husband!"

"So much for female bonding!"

"Or unity!"

"Or for us *Black women* surviving together!"

I try to reestablish some harmonious consensus by saying, "But couldn't an argument be made that Sula slept with Nell's husband to *strengthen* their bond?"

"Good luck making that argument."

*I don't need luck! I've got game!*

"Look, Dr. J, right here on page 144." Everyone turns to page 144. It is the part where Nell is confronting Sula about the affair. "'What did you take him for,'" the student reads, "'if you didn't love him, and why didn't you think about me?'"

Another student: "Page 145, first paragraph: 'And you didn't love me enough to leave him alone. To let him love me. You had to take him away.'"

And then others:

"Same page, right above that, Nell says, 'We were friends.'"

"Right below that Sula responds, 'Yes. Good friends.'"

"How is that not betrayal, Dr. J?"

"Yeah! How is that *not* betrayal?"

"Unless you're saying, Dr. J, that you think it'd be *okay* to sleep with your friend's wife?"

"Is *that* what you're saying, *Dr. J*?"

There is a section in my effective teaching book about the importance of knowing when to cede arguments even if it means being wrong, which conflicts with the section in my brain about the importance of winning all arguments, at all costs. Last semester, when discussing *Sula*, this conflict did not come into play, as everyone understood Sula's belief that her bond with Nell should have been capable of the ultimate forgiveness. I finished that class by reciting another of my rehearsed strong sentences: "Their historic support of one another, even in the face of what might be considered personal failings and lapses of judgment, is what makes women the backbone of the Black community, the primary reason, perhaps, for its survival." That evening, when Brenda asked how class went, I said, "Brilliantly!" When she asks me tonight, I say, "I won an argument!"

"About what?"

"Relationships."

"What about them?"

"Oh, you know, betrayals, affairs, lies. Stuff like that. I won't bore you with the details." I rise to get a beer and over my shoulder ask how was her class.

"I must admit," she replies, "it was amazing."

Better than amazing, I imagine, when she tells me she has reached the segment on the murals Zimbabwean women paint on the exteriors of their clay homes, the subject of her African art history dissertation. Six years earlier, I had been fortunate to accompany her to Zimbabwe while she conducted her field research, though we were both unfortunate to discover that, upon our arrival, we were no longer Black.

According to that country's race rules, we were, by virtue of the evident milk in our coffee, "Colored." Coloreds, generally speaking, on account of having benefited from centuries of apartheid rule, were despised by Blacks, which meant, generally speaking, Blacks despised us. We felt their animosity on a daily basis, usually in the form of sneers and lost hotel and restaurant reservations, but sometimes with verbal insults. Being treated so poorly was making me defensive and bitter; I mentioned this once to a taxi driver who'd asked if we were enjoying his country. "It's not surprising you feel this way," he responded. "Coloreds are defensive and bitter people."

"I'm *not* Colored," I said.

"They are disagreeable too."

I faced Brenda and mumbled, "This is fucked up."

"They are also profane," the driver added.

"And *violent*," I snapped, but later that evening, after I had calmed down, I wished I had instead asked him if he thought Coloreds shared his opinions of themselves. They did not, of course, no more than Black Americans consider themselves to be lazy, angry, and thievish, as is the opinion of many white Americans. I thought of how white Americans would see the absurdity of these and other racial stereotypes if they suddenly discovered they were Black in the way Brenda and I suddenly discovered we were not. If I ever taught Black literature at a predominately white college, I told myself, it would be a fun idea to explore.

And it is. I just have to eliminate making mistakes, or at least, per my book on teaching, to own up to them, as I am about to do now. "It is not true," I tell my students, "as I regrettably said during our last class, that I would have no problem sleeping with my friend's wife." What I should have said, I explain, is that Black women have historically relied on one another to summon the strength necessary to overcome obstacles, including those of their own making.

I lean into the notion of Black women summoning strength with our next book, Alice Walker's *The Color Purple*. By its conclusion, when Celie, the main character, triumphantly overcomes an abusive husband to be both financially and spiritually whole, the students are primed with thoughts of Black women's liberty and self-determination. It is a smooth transition from there to Zora Neale Hurston's *Their Eyes Were Watching God*, which lends itself to some spontaneous and much-improved finger-pointing as I declare, after the heroine survives three bad marriages to live on her own terms, that "Janie's strength is *your* inheritance!" and "Her tenacity is *your* birthright!" All of which is to say I am balling up in here, and there is consensus on this point: Black women, generally speaking, are badasses.

Black men, however, have been taking a hit. Their behavior toward Black women has ranged from unpleasant to heinous, and Bigger Thomas, the protagonist of our next book, *Native Son*, will do them no favors.

I once felt he was doing me one, though, by giving voice to our shared experiences. Like me, Bigger was born in a Chicago housing project and dropped out of school in his teens. We both dabbled in petty crimes and dreamed of committing grand ones. We were both even hired to work for rich white people, him as a chauffeur for a real estate tycoon, me as a lab-equipment cleaner in a private hospital. Spending all day working for rich white people and then returning to the ghetto crystallized for Bigger and me our stark disadvantages. Sometimes, while elbow-deep in human waste and disinfectant, I would look around at those rich white doctors and seethe. What I wanted to do, in moments like those, was kill all them honkies.

Bigger did—not all of them, of course, but a significant one, Mary, the daughter of his employer. She had gotten drunk one night while out on the town, and after Bigger drove her home he helped her to her bedroom. Mary's mother, who was blind, came to check on her after hearing slurred speech. A Black man in a drunk, slurring white woman's bedroom, Bigger knew, was not ideal. As Mary's mother grew nearer, Bigger panicked and pressed a pillow against Mary's face to keep her quiet. Her slurring stopped, her mother retreated, and, just like that, for Mary's breathing had stopped too, Bigger was a murderer. An accidental one, to be sure, though his creator, not God but the author Richard Wright, would have readers believe there was an inevitability to his actions, that being a poor, Black male meant being without choices, a victim of racism's brutal forces with no capacity to confront or defeat them. So Bigger had nothing to lose, he felt, especially after shoving Mary's lifeless body into the basement furnace, in murdering his Black girlfriend too. This all made sense to me—until, that is, a Bigger Thomas wannabe murdered my close friend after nearly murdering me and I discovered I had choices after all. I left the ghetto and returned to school.

But even as my future unfolded with promise, I still felt a kinship with Bigger. It continued to ring true to me in some vague way that Black folks, as he insisted, were "whipped before they are born," although I read these words as a flourishing college student. Most of my own college students claim to see a truth in these words too, specifically, they say, regarding people of Bigger's background. Last year, when my Black student sided with this majority in his class, I thought, *So much for having the answers in advance of the exam*. He was incorrect, too, along with his like-minded peers in both classes, in saying that I was the exception after I explained I share much of Bigger's background. Bigger, of course, was the exception. He was also a straw man, and in this way he serves my purpose; the refutation of straw men, says my teaching book, can bolster a course's theme. And the perfect refuter of Bigger Thomas is the protagonist of our final book, Ralph Ellison's *Invisible Man*.

*Invisible Man* tells the story of a naive southerner who moves North and over time learns to match wits with everyone from racists and communists to Black sellouts and Black nationalists. Faced with waves of adversity, his ability to improvise—the most important Black survival strategy, perhaps, of them all—leaves my students enthralled. The notion that he is symbolic of African Americans' heroic journey from slavery to freedom must have been percolating just below my students' level of consciousness, because when I mentioned it, they readily agreed. By novel's end, as the protagonist breaks into fits of laughter while reflecting on the *advantages* of being the hunted rather than the hunter, of being, in other words, the tactical matador instead of the raging bull, the idea of Bigger Thomas as a Black archetype has lost its hold on my students.

This had been *Invisible Man*'s effect on me too. I first read it in graduate school, and for months afterward I felt as if I had been lobotomized along with the novel's protagonist. "Who am I?" he muses, as he awakes from that procedure, a third of the way through the novel. "Maybe I was just this blackness and bewilderment and pain, but that seemed less like a suitable answer than something I read somewhere." This was a direct blow to my internalized definition of blackness, and then, a few months later, as Brenda and I were in Zimbabwe being stripped of our race, my externalized definition of blackness took a direct blow too. When I returned to the States, I reread the invisible man's post-lobotomy musings; it was then that passages that I had highlighted took on deeper resonance:

> *I feel, feel suddenly that I have become more human.*
>
> *For the first time, lying there in the dark, I could glimpse the possibility of being more than a member of a race.*
>
> *Why waste your time creating a conscience for something that doesn't exist? For you see, blood and skin do not think!*
>
> *Our task is that of making ourselves individuals. . . . We create the race by creating ourselves and then to our great astonishment we will have created something more important. We will have created a culture.*

"The culture we have created," I say at the end of our final class, "is the means by which our race is embodied, not, contrary to the rules of this country, the blood in our veins or the color of our skin." This is my strongest sentence, one with which I brought last year's class to a close. But after delivering it this time, as the students thank me and begin to rise and gather their belongings, I elevate my game.

"One last thing," I say, "before you go."

I reach beneath my desk to retrieve a small paper bag, from which I remove a dropper and, I swear to them, the same cup of milk from the first day of the semester. "Per course rules," I say, over scattered laughter, "your blackness lasts only for the duration of the course. It will be undone," I add, "once I find and remove that drop of coffee." My first futile attempts bring more laughter, as well as some applause. But then, slowly, the room quiets. They all nod. They see.

Hugs abound.

## STOPPED BY THE POLICE

After getting word of a local car dealer's motto, "No Credit, No Job, No Problem," and not wanting to miss out on the limited-time-only 40 percent interest rate, I landed a sweet Lincoln Continental, only seventeen years old, like me. Cruising my strip of ghetto, I was indisputably *the Man*, eliciting fist pumps from the brothers, finger waves from the ladies, and harassment from the police. Every time a squad car pulled up behind me, swirling its unholy lights, I feared, I must say, for my life. But no more. In the decades since those days, I learned, as the vast majority of Blacks at some point learn, how to play the police like fiddles.

My first steps to that end were to leave my teens, my Lincoln, and my ghetto, as well as to perfect versions of this script: *Yes, officer. No, officer. Thank you, officer, for reminding me to renew my registration when it expires.* When I had sons of driving age, I knew I would teach these scripts to them, as my father had to me and my brothers, being sure to stress that if they were stopped by the police, or anyone, for that matter, with a lethal weapon, to do as they were told and to keep their hands in plain view. Many African Americans find this discussion—commonly referred to as "The Talk"—to be an offensive and heartrending burden, but I prefer to think of it as one of the many survival strategies we have devised to outwit our oppressors.

This one I devised on my own: when driving excessively above highway speed limits, I try to do so only in the company of other excessive speeders, thereby reducing my odds of being easy prey for state troopers. This has worked well. Still, I have been led to believe radars can detect both velocity and pigmentation, given the number of occasions I have been plucked from these lawless caravans. But one recent time it happened, rather than deliver a survivors' script, I delivered a script of white privilege, on loan to me by my friend John, sitting to my right. "What horseshit," he'd said, upon spotting the patrol car emerge from the brush we whizzed by. "Five drivers speeding and of course he'll stop *you*."

Maybe not, I thought, if some of the other drivers were also Black, the odds of which were slim; we were on Cape Cod, a region not exactly known for clusters of Negroes. I looked in my rearview mirror, watched the officer circumvent the car speeding behind me before merging back into my lane. Its lights popped on. I braked and made my way to the shoulder, taking a final glimpse at my cohorts as they—laughing, I imagined—barreled unimpeded toward their destinations.

A moment later, the officer stood at my door peering through my lowered window. If he had any concerns of a white male bearing witness to his racial profiling, he expressed them only with a grin. "Know why I stopped you?" he asked.

I said, "I have my suspicions."

"You were speeding."

"As were the four other drivers you *didn't* stop."

"Well, I couldn't stop you all, could I?"

"So why did you stop *me*?"

"Because," he said, side-eyeing John, "you were going the fastest."

"But how could I have been going faster than the car directly in front of me?"

"Like this." He walked forward at a rapid clip, representing, he said over his shoulder, the car directly in front of me, and then, representing me, I assumed, for now he was too far away for me to hear him, by sprinting. Before he made his way back to me, John whispered, "No chance in hell this guy's giving you a ticket."

"Zero," I responded.

Back at my window, slightly out of breath, the officer asked, "See what I mean?"

I said, "What horseshit."

"*Easy*, mister. I didn't say I was giving you a ticket. Just *take it easy*." He demanded my license and registration. I handed them over. He returned to his vehicle, I assumed to search for my outstanding warrants.

I had none, of course. Other than speeding while Black, I was irreproachable, since faithfully following the law, as I would also teach my sons, was a survival strategy too. I laughed as I had imagined the escapees doing, and then, a short while later, as I pulled back onto the highway with only a written warning, I laughed some more. I owed it to

myself, this laughter, to make up for all the times, after being stopped by police, there had been none. A catalog of
these stops played in my mind—replete with frisks, searches,
handcuffing, threats, and interrogations—before lingering
on one in particular.

Technically, I had not been stopped. Nor had I been
speeding or cruising a ghetto. I was Black, nonetheless, and
in a sweet luxury car. The car was a Volvo S70 and it was only
two years old, like my son Adrian, who was in the back seat
refusing to be lulled asleep by an afternoon drive. A Lincoln
Continental, I believed, would have instantly done the trick
with its legendary suspension system, but in an effort to be a
responsible parent I had purchased the Volvo for its legendary
safety features. Unfortunately, those safety features offered
no protection against menacing cops. I had attracted one
soon after I left home, and now, several minutes later, as I
wound through residential streets of small-town Massachusetts, he continued to match my every move.

At one point, to prove to myself I was actually being followed and not just paranoid or having a flashback, I pulled
into a gas station. The officer pulled in behind me. I crept
past the pumps and turned toward the street, where, as luck
would have it, there was room for only one car to merge into
the flow of vehicles. The officer ended up three cars back, but
only for as long as it took for a break in the oncoming traffic,
at which point he swooped around the cars separating us and
retook his position on my bumper. Had I been a teenager, I
would have been convulsing with fear. I was thirty-eight,
though, and convulsing with rage. For while I no longer

thought of myself as *the Man*, I very much thought of myself as *a Man*—a Man who had fathered a Son, and I refused, in that moment, to be harassed by the police in his presence. I slammed on the brakes, threw my car in park, and then shoved open my door and climbed out, fully prepared to die.

But not without witnesses. I had purposefully driven to a mall and beelined for its main entrance, where I knew there would be shoppers pushing out of its revolving doors. Perhaps some of them, like me, expected to hear a barrage of gunfire when my feet hit the pavement, but the only sound was of my straining voice. *"What the hell are you doing?"* I yelled, facing the now idling cruiser, ten feet away. *"Why the hell are you following me?"* The officer sat motionless behind his wheel, even as I continued to yell, and then I began to gesticulate, at him, yes, but also to draw more attention from onlookers. A small crowd had indeed formed that I was not yet aware of; I was fixated on the cop, waiting for him to burst from his vehicle, but he remained inside, so I continued to yell and gesticulate, ceasing only when he floored his engine and tore past me, his face, I had glimpsed, twisted into a frown that haunts me still. But this haunts me more: the thought of my son not having a father because I had allowed a cop to *play me*. I vowed that day that if I were ever to lose my life at the hands of the police, it would not be, beyond the mere color of my skin, with my assistance.

And yet, there I had been, ten years later in the car with John, antagonizing a state trooper. Even as I drove away laughing, I knew that I had engaged in needlessly risky behavior, for surely, had that behavior motivated the trooper to do me harm, he would not have been dissuaded by my white passenger. The success rate of Black survival strategies, no matter how flawlessly employed, is not 100 percent; the success rate of antagonizing a white cop is far less. I renewed my vow to faithfully adhere to a tried-and-true script the next time I was pulled over. Luckily, that would not be for another five years.

My luck ended while I was en route to the campus where I taught for a faculty committee meeting. I had gotten a late start, and so I knew that to make it on time, I would have to break all my prior speeding records, beginning on the residential streets between my house and the highway. I was hightailing it down one such street when its bend straightened to reveal an officer standing next to his parked squad car, his radar gun raised, computing my speed and complexion. In violation on both counts, I slowed to a stop even before being motioned to do so. I put the car in park, cut the engine, and lowered the driver's window. I had just placed my hands high on the steering wheel when the officer arrived at my side.

"Do you have any idea," he began, "how fast you were going?"

"No, sir."

"Guess."

"A little over thirty?"

He said, *"Sixty-eight."*

"Sixty-eight?"

"What's the rush?" he asked, but before I could respond, he said, "Nice car."

It wasn't *nice*. It was *sweet*, and brand new: an Audi Q5 with all the bells and whistles. "Thank you, officer."

"Is it yours?"

"Yes, sir."

"How long you had it?"

"Three days, sir."

He glanced at the passenger seat where, unfortunately, there was a brown satchel instead of a white person. "What brings you to this neighborhood?"

"I live here, officer."

"Where?"

"Just around the corner."

"Where, *exactly*?"

I told him. Looking skeptical, he asked for my license. I handed it to him. He studied it for a long time, occasionally glancing from it to me, making sure, I supposed, that I was the person in the photo. Or possibly my address was requiring a recalibration of his expectations, as well as some soul-searching and maybe even a little guilt that I hoped would be to my benefit, since he must have assumed that I was speeding through this wealthy white town in a stolen car, racing back to some ghetto where I would be, indisputably, *the Man*. Now he had to allow for the possibility that I already was.

He lowered my license before saying, "Registration."

I retrieved it, very slowly, from the glove compartment. He took it and without a word headed to his car.

As I waited, I texted the committee chair to say that I would be late. And then, by way of the perfect excuse, I added, "Stopped by the police." I figured he would relay my text to our colleagues, and I was right; when I arrived thirty minutes later, I was greeted with cries of outrage and pity. But as soon as everyone settled down, I set them straight. "I was caught driving in a residential area," I explained, "thirty miles an hour over the speed limit." I paused to let the fact of my guilt sink in before revealing my triumph. "And all I have to show for it," I said, "is a ticket."

## LOST

A late-to-be-home child can induce high anxiety in parents, and if the lateness occurs at night, and the child is a Black male teenager, the high anxiety can run amok. Brenda disagreed that the time for high anxiety had been reached, and since her mind is run amok–proof, I alone offered troubling scenarios to explain Adrian's absence before I managed to *get a grip* because what likely happened was that during theater practice, our clumsy fourteen-year-old had stumbled off the stage, been knocked unconscious, and was now headed to the hospital in the care of competent and loving EMTs. Brenda would appreciate this latest scenario, I thought, based on her displeasure with my bleaker ones.

"Did I ever tell you," I began, "that once, when I was fourteen, I had a concussion?"

She looked up from her laptop, her fingers hovering above the keys.

"Concussions," I continued, "run on my side of the family."

"And?"

"The Walker cranium, you see, is uncommonly delicate."

"You're telling me this why?"

I offered my stumble theory. A beat passed before she looked back at her laptop and resumed typing. We were sitting at the kitchen island, surrounded by clocks: on the microwave, the stove, the cable box beneath the small countertop TV, our phones, which lay before us, not beeping, buzzing, or ringing. It was, by unanimous consent, 12:31 AM. Adrian had said he would be home at around 9:30 PM. But he had offered the caveat that, because this was the final rehearsal before tomorrow's big performance, they might run a little late.

Three hours was not a little. Granted, the theater teacher was a perfectionist, and none of the actors, from the performances we had seen, were Broadway bound, but after a while you just have to say it is what it is and be done. That had been my first thought: the exasperated teacher throwing up her hands to call it a wrap and then Adrian bumming a ride from a friend. Only I pictured this friend to be a Black male teenager too. Then I pictured him being stopped by a white cop, and because he had not been taught to put his hands high on the wheel and say *Yes, officer. No, officer. Thank you, officer, for reminding me to renew my registration when it expires*, he gestured aggressively while complaining about being racially profiled. Mercifully, that was as far as I got with that scenario before reminding myself that Adrian was the only Black student in the theater program, and one of the few at his school.

So I replaced the Black friend with two Jewish ones because I have never ceased to be tormented by the tragic story of Andrew Goodman, James Chaney, and Michael Schwerner. The Ku Klux Klan murdered the young interracial trio in

1964, and it would be three long months before their bodies were found buried beneath an earthen dam. I could not imagine, though Lord knows I have tried, their parent's heartbreak when someone bearing the devastating news rang their doorbell. And then I could imagine it because, at 12:39 AM, someone rang ours.

I teleported to the living room. Our front door was made with etched glass, and so before I opened it I could see a lone figure on the porch, the overhead light too dim to reveal if it was Adrian or a detective to explain why it was not.

It was Adrian, alive, apparently unharmed, and looking oddly flushed for a cool fall evening. He shuffled into the room beneath the massive backpack that nearly toppled him as he leaned over to release it from his shoulders. I took in the fact of his presence, my heart flooding with love and relief, but, having inherited my father's parenting style, I resisted the urge to embrace him in favor of yelling. "*Boy*, what took you so long? Your *mother* was worried sick about you!"

He looked at her and apologized.

"It's okay, baby," Brenda said as she joined us. She gave him my hug.

I gave him more of my father. "No, it's *not* okay! *You should have called!*"

"I was *going* to," he said, "but my phone had died."

Brenda ruffled his hair. "Don't worry about it," she said, smiling. "It happens."

"Happens my derriere!" I said. "Derriere" was one of my father's favorite words, the height of profanity for a man who never cursed. He also never spared the rod, not even when I was fourteen; had he and I been cast in this drama, his belt would have been slithering from his pants right about now. Feeling sorry for my younger self, I patted my back, which is to say Adrian's. "Next time, son," I said, "so that your poor mother isn't anxious, just borrow someone's phone."

"I couldn't," he said. He stepped into the kitchen and took a glass from the cupboard. As he filled it with tap water, he explained that after everyone had left the theater and headed for the school's exit, he realized he had forgotten his phone backstage. He returned for it, which was when he discovered the battery had died. By the time he got to the parking lot, everyone was gone.

"Everyone," I corrected him, "except for whoever drove you home."

He drank some water before correcting me: "No one drove me home."

I looked at Brenda, who seemed to be turning pale, indicating, I gathered, that the point of high anxiety had been reached.

She said, "You mean . . . ?"

I said, "So . . . how . . . ?"

She said, "Are you telling us . . . ?"

I added, ". . . did . . . you . . . um . . . you . . . ?"

He said, "I walked!"

His school was a fifteen-minute drive away. That translated, according to MapQuest, to a ninety-minute walk, give or take another hour for a five-foot, ninety-pound boy carrying a backpack the size of a dresser. It was an extraordinary act of physical endurance, one of which he was proud, judging from his grin. And I would have praised him for it had I not been thinking of how a five-foot, ninety-pound Black boy carrying an enormous backpack through a very white and very wealthy small town in the middle of the night translated, according to America, to a six-foot, two-hundred-pound burglar with a bag full of loot. Then my running-amok mind asked itself this horrifying question: *What if he'd gotten lost?*

"I got lost," Adrian said.

I teleported to the liquor cabinet. As I removed a mug and bottle of Scotch, I casually asked over my shoulder, "You didn't, by chance, stop at someone's house to ask for directions, did you?"

"Well, I was *about* to," he said, "but then I figured out how to get to Main Street."

We lived on Main Street. It spanned our entire town. In a visit there in 1942, Eleanor Roosevelt declared it "the most beautiful street in America," primarily because its wide expanse was lined with massive elms, and behind many of those massive elms were multimillion-dollar estates, and behind many of those multimillion-dollar estates, I had glimpsed now and then, were horses. Most of the homes on our end of Main Street were considerably more modest in size, price, and pets, but they were by no means inexpensive, and their occupants, perhaps even more so than the multimillion-dollar-estate occupants, upon being roused from sleep by a Black person at the door, would have been petrified, possibly hostile, and maybe even, like Theodore Paul Wafer, moved to commit murder.

The Black person Theodore Paul Wafer murdered was a

nineteen-year-old named Renisha McBride. A year earlier, in 2013, McBride crashed her car while traveling through Dearborn Heights, Michigan, a small town that was 85 percent white—10 percent less white than where we lived. Her car was totaled, but she was uninjured enough to walk in search of assistance. At around 4:30 AM, she knocked on Wafer's door. Wafer, after opening it and seeing a lone girl looking discombobulated and, I imagine, relieved, raised his shotgun and unloaded it in her face. He feared she was a burglar, he later claimed, which did not deter the authorities from charging him with second-degree murder, manslaughter, and possession of a firearm during the commission of a crime. He was convicted on all counts.

Charged with manslaughter but not convicted was Randall Kerrick, the Charlotte, North Carolina, police officer who just a few months prior to McBride's death killed a Black man named Jonathan Ferrell. Like McBride, Ferrell had crashed his car in the night, and he too had gone on foot searching for assistance, stopping for it at a random house not far from his immobilized vehicle. The lethal weapon this homeowner wielded was not a shotgun but a phone. She used it to call 911, reporting a burglary in progress at her residence. Soon afterward, Officer Kerrick arrived on the scene, whereupon he shot Ferrell twelve times, a bullet for every two years of his life.

In 2023, a sixteen-year-old Black child in Kansas City, Missouri, named Ralph Yarl would be shot in the head by a white homeowner after mistakenly going to the wrong address in search of his younger brother. But because this would not happen for nine years, I could not acknowledge it with wide eyes when I returned to the kitchen with my mug of Scotch, so I only acknowledged what had happened to McBride and Ferrell in this manner.

Later that night, I acknowledged what happened to them again with a bout of insomnia, which gave me more than enough time to consider this irony: Brenda and I had busted our derrieres to raise our sons in a community where it was safe for them to walk its streets at night, which, by dint of their blackness, meant it was not safe for them to walk its streets at night. What was worse was that Adrian had *felt* safe, which made him *less* safe, because it never dawned on him that stopping at a house to seek help could have been to his peril. And maybe this was worst of all: despite the grim turn this evening could have taken, I continued to believe that Brenda and I had done the right thing by raising our sons to never doubt, not for a second, that they, like their white classmates, could leave the grounds of their high school on foot, in the middle of the night, and make it home alive. The weight of a sixty-pound backpack, it seemed to me, was enough for a child to carry.

And yet, I had a growing suspicion we should have done things differently.

I gently shook Brenda's shoulder, waking her. "What?" she muttered. "What's wrong?"

"I think," I whispered, "we fucked up."

"What are you talking about?"

"The boys," I said. "We should have taught them, from the time they were toddlers, that their lives were at risk."

She lifted her head off her pillow, I believe; it was too dark to know for sure. "What time is it?" she asked.

"Two o'clock? Two thirty? Maybe three."

A spark of light illuminated her face as she tapped her Fitbit. "It's after four!"

"Is that by unanimous consensus, or . . ."

"Have you slept at all?"

"No."

"You need to."

"*Seriously?* You're talking about *sleep* when our sons, thanks to us, although the bulk of the blame, let's be honest here, is yours, are *clueless.*"

"Clueless about what?"

"What it *means* to be Black."

"Jerald, please. I need to get a little more sleep."

"Adrian could have been *killed* last night!"

"We've been over this."

We had, it was true, but not from every conceivable angle. Shortly before she'd fallen asleep, I had floated some worst-case scenarios that might have befallen to Adrian, after each of which she redirected my thoughts to two important facts: he was home, and he was safe. The thing to do, she urged me, was to be grateful. Ultimately, I agreed. But a lot had changed since then: namely, my reassessment of our parenting.

"The point I'm making," I continued, "is that he would have *known* not to leave the school if we'd raised him with more racial awareness."

"He has plenty of racial awareness," she said. "What he

doesn't have is racial paranoia. Like the kind," she added, "that runs on your side of the family."

The Walker racism detector, it was true, was uncommonly delicate.

My father's was the exception. To him, racism was just another of life's challenges to be confronted and overcome, not unlike the accident he'd had when he was twelve that had cost him his sight. In my twenties, as I was experimenting with Black nationalism, it struck me that my father's blindness was a metaphor for his approach to race, the way he had failed to situate it as the albatross of our lives, and how, if he had been able to look in a mirror, he would have seen, first and foremost, a Black man looking back.

A curious thing, though; when I became a father (i.e., him), I wondered if what I had considered to be metaphorical blindness was really a kind of sight, because suddenly what I wanted more than anything for my children was what he had wanted for his: identities formed from within—for our mirrors, in other words, to first and foremost reflect humans. It was fair to say that Brenda and I had achieved this goal. And yet, heaven help us, our oldest son was wandering around a white town in the middle of the night, *lost*. This metaphor did not escape me either.

In a few hours, before Adrian and Dorian left for school, I confirmed that their phones were charged, and that night, as they were readying for bed, I confirmed that their phones were charging. As if the likelihood of their safety could be measured in battery cells. As if their continued existence was based on their ability to reach their parents at a moment's notice. Which, I assured them, they could. *Call if you need us!* became my mantra, said every time they headed out the door. But that sentence never carried more significance than the day I said it to them four and six years later, when Adrian, and then Dorian, left for college.

Now their late-to-be-homeness is perpetual. So, too, is my high anxiety, especially when they do not contact us for days on end. This has not been the case so much with Adrian, who is very good about staying in touch, even if only by text, but Dorian, it seems, is determined to have my high anxiety run amok. It was close to doing so after one particularly long stretch of not hearing from him when he suddenly called. Brenda put her phone on speaker as he gave updates about his classes, new friends he had made, and how he was adapting to living in a large urban city. He never sounded happier. He had even found a solution, he said, for the insomnia I had bequeathed him.

"I go for long walks," he said.

Brenda and I looked at each other.

"Last night, for instance," he continued, "I went to bed at around eleven, but I was still wide awake at two, so I got dressed and went out for a few hours."

"A few hours?" Brenda repeated.

"Yeah," he said, chuckling. "That was a lot longer than I'd planned."

*Wait for it*, I thought . . .

"I got lost," he said.

I teleported to the future, some undetermined time when

I would stress to him the dangers of what he had done, particularly for a Black male. To spare his poor mother worry, I would say, he should reconsider such nocturnal excursions. Right now, however, I heeded Brenda's stern expression, which was instructing me to focus on the fact that he had made it back to his dorm safe and sound. *Be grateful for this*, her eyes implored me, and I was.

And maybe I was a little envious too. In a few hours, after I had laid awake considering the bad outcomes he had averted, I pictured myself wandering around in the middle of the night, fearing no one, and being oblivious to causing fear, for I was just a human being out for a stroll, unsure, at times, of where I was and of where I was going, and largely unconcerned. What does it feel like, I wondered, for a Black man to experience such a thing? Freedom? Bliss? Nothing at all? I do not know. I simply, for the life of me, cannot imagine it. Though Lord knows I've tried.

## GOOD HELP

The contractor, having reached a high level of comfort with our acquaintance, aided, no doubt, by my daily offerings of Gatorade to him and his crew, as well as by my easy laughter at his off-color jokes, gently placed a hand on my shoulder, seemingly cleared away a hint of emotion from his voice, and confessed he used to be a racist. He then relayed a story about how, many years ago, when he was down on his luck, battling alcoholism, obesity, and depression, a counselor at his homeless shelter talked him out of ending it all, convincing him he was a child of God, worthy of love and redemption. "And to think," he added, suddenly looking away, but not before shedding a single tear, "that the man God sent to save me was a nigger."

I was shocked, needless to say, as I had never seen a contractor cry. I pretended not to have noticed, like I pretended not to have heard the slur, which, given his brand of humor, had not shocked me at all, and which I had taken, even more than his tear, as evidence of his sincerity. He had spoken to me as unguardedly as one would to a friend. But he was fortunate I was not the kind of person who took language out of context, or who was especially sensitive to language at all, or who, after hiring a contractor, cared about much more than the quality of the work. And his was *superb*.

This was an uncommon experience for me; in decades of homeownership, I had not been very successful in finding good help. I had not, in fact, found him. He had been referred to me by my insurance company after a microburst wreaked havoc on our new addition. When it formed, the snapping of timber sent me rushing to our family room to look out the window where several massive pines, uprooted and fast approaching, sent me running for my life. The sound of the impact was tremendous! I turned to see branches protruding through the ceiling, a wall cracked and buckled, furniture littered with sheetrock and glass. I also saw, in my mind's eye, a construction crew botching the repairs. But I did not, not in my wildest imagination, see a highly skilled worker among them.

Then again, I also had not imagined seeing a highly skilled worker installing a bluestone patio in my backyard, and yet, only a year prior, there one was. I had chanced upon his services after a Google search, selecting him over countless others based solely on a hunch derived from his ancient, withered appearance; *this old-timer*, I thought, *knows his stuff*. And by *his stuff*, to be clear, I meant masonry, as opposed to, say, Negro-ry, so I did not anticipate keen insight into the latter when one day, as I stood admiring his craftsmanship, he broached the subject. "I don't mean no disrespect by this," he began, "but I'm just puzzled, you know, by your race. If you don't mind me asking, what are you?"

"I don't mind at all," I said. "I'm Black."

"Black *what* though?" he responded. "From where?"

"From a place far, far away called 'Chicago.'"

"Chicago?" he exclaimed. "No shit?"

"None whatsoever."

"I was certain you were foreign."

"Like Barack Obama?" I asked, smiling.

Not smiling, he said, "Exactly."

"Nope, I'm just a regular Black, like Michelle. Been one now for fifty-seven years."

"You're *fifty-seven*? Me too!"

We stared at each other in wonder. I had taken him to be eighty. He insisted I did not look a day over forty. "Well," I began, "you know what they say?"

"What's that?"

"Black don't crack!"

He looked puzzled.

"Our skin," I said. "As we age, it doesn't crack. With wrinkles."

"Unless," he noted, "you're *on* crack."

"That would be an exception, yes."

"A lot of regular Blacks *are* on it, as you obviously know. But you're clearly not to be able to afford this expensive house. That's why I thought you were from somewhere else." He removed his cap, wiped his forearm across his brow. "So, what do you do for a living?"

I glanced over my shoulders, then leaned toward him and whispered, "I *sell* crack."

He frowned, perhaps believing that I was mocking him,

which I was and which I instantly regretted; the patio was turning out beautifully and I had hoped to hire him to build a firepit. But when I mentioned it the next day, it was as I'd feared; "I'm *booked*," he said, "for the foreseeable future."

That was just as well. In the hot summer sun, the patio heated up like a griddle and was tough to use. And when we used it in the evening, mosquitoes ate us alive. What we really needed, I decided, was a screened gazebo. There was a company that made them not far from where we lived. I completed a form on its website and a few hours later the owner called to set up a date to meet at his office.

When Brenda and I arrived, he looked up from his desk and did a double take, as if standing before him were two Black people there to buy a gazebo. Which could not be the case, he must have determined, since gazebos, as he explained after leading us outside to view the models, cost a lot of money. "Even *that* little number," he said, pointing to his right, "demands a pretty penny."

I looked to his right. "We don't need a chicken coop," I said.

"That's not a *chicken coop*. It's our most *affordable* gazebo."

Brenda gestured toward one looming over it. "That's more of what we have in mind."

"*That*," he said, "is our most *expensive* model."

"We'd like to see it," she said.

"Well . . . okay," he replied. "But just so you know, we don't finance."

"How about layaway?" I deadpanned.

He snorted. "We don't do that here."

"Rent to own?"

"Afraid not," he said.

"What about stilts?"

"Stilts?"

Our backyard, I explained, sloped into the woods. We wanted the gazebo to rise from the woods on stilts. He chuckled before glancing toward the street, expecting, maybe, the host of some prank show to emerge from a parked van. When one did not, he said, "You can't put a gazebo on stilts."

I took out my phone and showed him a photo I had gotten from the internet of a gazebo rising from the woods on stilts. There was a bridge connecting it to the yard. "Plus the bridge," I said.

He told us he would have to consult an engineer, and then we went back to his office to schedule a site visit I knew would not be kept. That was okay by me. I had decided at the chicken coop not to force my money on this racist when there were plenty of other ones eager to have it, like the next gazebo builder I contacted, who insisted he wasn't a racist even before I offered him Gatorade. All I had offered him was a look at my photo of a gazebo on stilts rising from the woods.

"Plus the bridge?" he asked.

I said, "Plus the bridge."

"No problem." Then he turned his attention to Brenda. "I just want to say that I enjoy working for people of the Indian persuasion."

"Do you?" Brenda responded. "That's nice."

"I have found many of your people," he continued, "to be polite and well-mannered, like the woman I recently did a job for across town, who you very closely resemble. Your sister, maybe?"

"My sister doesn't live in this town," Brenda responded, although, likely to spare him embarrassment, she did not say they weren't Indian.

"They're not Indian," I said.

He faced me, cheeks and neck reddening.

"Sorry," I continued. "They're just regular Blacks."

"Regular, irregular," he stammered, "Puerto Rican, Mexican, Asian, or Jew, people are people, as far as I'm concerned. Whatever someone is don't matter to me."

What did matter to him, it seemed, given his exorbitant quote, was including a minority-people-are-people surcharge. That must have also mattered to the next two contractors from whom I also received exorbitant quotes, which almost made me long for the contractor who had built our addition. Not only were his rates below market value, but he was Black, and I like to support Black-owned businesses, especially when doing so saves me money. It was too bad he had made so many mistakes, thereby confirming a hunch I'd had upon meeting him, derived not from his race, as he would later accuse me, but from his three missing fingers. *This guy*, I thought, *will fuck up some shit*. And by *fuck up some shit*, to be clear, I meant misaligning a window or door, as opposed to, say, the entire structure.

That happened while Brenda, our sons, and I were attending *Hamilton*: an exterior wall framed two feet too high, which, to accommodate the minimally required roof pitch, resulted in the framing of the opposing wall being *eight* feet too high, so that in the time it took the colonies to be transformed into a nation, our Cape Cod had been transformed into a mid-century modern. Good thing I had always wanted one. I did not anticipate being as lucky with future mistakes, however, and so for the next nine months of construction, I roamed the premises, pointing out all that I suspected or knew to be wrong. Eventually the contractor grew frustrated with my oversight, one day even losing his temper. I had just raised concerns about the location of ductwork. "Another *word* out of you," he snapped, "and I *swear* I'll quit!"

"But you must concede," I said, attempting to reason with him, "that the ductwork should have been installed in the crawl space, per the plans, and not on the ceiling?"

"I will concede that," he responded, "if *you* concede that you wouldn't be so critical if I wasn't Black!"

That was true. Had he not been Black, I would have fired him long ago without a word. Maybe not the day of the framing mistake, but surely the day of the plumbing mistake, or the flooring mistake, or the siding mistake. I had been extralenient because of his race, I realized, a lapse in judgment that I remedied a year later after the addition was destroyed by the microburst. When the insurance agent asked if I would like to rehire the contractor who had built it, I declined. "I'll use whoever you send," I said, "as long as they know their stuff." And, to be clear, by *their stuff* I meant home repair, as opposed to, say, white guilt.

The contractor she sent knew both. It was after I had praised the newly installed roof that he confessed his racist

past, the hard times he had endured that rendered him sui-
cidal, and the Black counselor who had convinced him not to
end his life. Then he'd turned away, a tear on his cheek, and
gone silent. A few seconds passed before I gently rested a
hand on his shoulder, as he had on mine a moment earlier. "I
just want you to know," I said, "in all sincerity, that you do
superb work. Without question, you are the most skilled
contractor, the absolute finest, I have ever known."

He faced me again. His eyes were still moist, as if soon
more tears would fall, convincing me, in hindsight, that he
had hoped to be counseled again. Maybe he had wanted me to
urge him not to berate himself for his prior views on race. Or
he had wanted me to say that I, as a Black man, was personally thankful for his repentance. And as a bonus, which I believe he would have appreciated, I could have cautioned him
to be mindful of how he referred to Black people, especially in
our presence, for the next one who heard him say "nigger"
might take great offense. Yes, I later realized, he had wanted
help, the good kind that, alas, is hard to find.

# CRISIS

It was a mistake, I see now, to have worn a suit to the cannabis store. Compared to the people lined up near its entrance, I am decidedly overdressed, and under-tattooed. It also appears that I am the wrong age by approximately thirty-five years, which is how long it has been since I last bought pot. I have not missed pot very much, as it was never my favorite means of getting high; nor have I missed the dangers of what buying it entailed, chief among them the chance of arrest. Inconceivably, that chance largely no longer exists, and this, primarily, is why I am here. Society owes me, the way I see it, at least one stress-free drug deal.

But my suit is working against me. As soon as I leave my car, the customers in line cast me looks of disdain and suspicion, as if I am well, a *suit*, which, unfortunately, based on my assumption that suits would be the main clientele, was the impression I sought. After all, the website's interior photos are of a showroom worthy of a high-end jeweler: rows of display counters made of marble and topped with glass, inside of which awaited an array of gems. The building's exterior, however, is unassuming, intentionally so, most likely, located as it is on a street that is both commercial and residential; it *was* once a residence and its facade still resembles one, a ubiquitous New England cape landscaped with hollies, wisteria, and, on each side of its walkway, creeping dogwoods. Were the establishment's name not located on the two-car garage, one would never know this is the place to score your Maui Wowie flower or Lemon Disco popcorn buds.

The pot of my youth did not have such clever names. It was simply referred to as "the Fire," "the Bomb," or "That Good Shit." But it was often accompanied by a dealer's enticing claim, such as "One hit, brother, will *knock off your fucking balls*." Now, as I near sixty, it is important to me that my balls remain securely in place, and so before adding anything to my shopping cart I paid close attention to each item's description. The first one to really intrigue me was for a product called Island Punch: "Kick back and relax with these terpene-enhanced indica gummies," it read. "Their island-inspired flavor evokes a mouth-watering tropical punch, with hints of grape, orange, cherry, and pineapple." It also promised to make the consumer "relaxed, sleepy, and happy." I found this last part especially appealing, given the state of our nation's politics.

But . . . *gummies*? This was difficult for me to wrap my head around. I imagined my younger self on a street corner talking shit with my homies while we shared a package of chewables, no one coughing from taking a toke too greedily, no fingertips singed when the plant's last vestiges became embers, all of us increasing our odds of getting cavities instead of cancer. Once we were high and overcome with the munchies, would we have gone home, I wondered, to raid our refrigerators, or would we have satisfied our cravings by simply eating more gummies, a debaucherous loop of pleasure that ended in delirium and a tummy ache? Which made me wonder this: how many gummies were too many? I googled this question and read warnings that "chewable newbies" should take a conservative approach, which would have been good advice to receive when I was a "four-foot-long bong newbie." I returned to the website and read more descriptions, including several for topicals, vaporizers, beverages, concentrates, and tinctures. What a strange new world! But one thing about it was familiar, I discovered, after adding the gummies to my shopping cart and attempting to purchase them: the transaction had to be made in cash.

An hour ago, at around 2:00 PM, after donning my suit but forgoing, thank goodness, a tie, I drove to an ATM and withdrew eighty dollars. The package of gummies was just thirty-five dollars, but I was considering getting two. Even though I was not meeting some dealer in a dark alley, I was still a little uptight. I had already decided this would be a one-time venture.

But for a while there I was not sure it would even be that. When I reached the store, I sat in a long trail of idling cars, each inching its way from the street and into the driveway that led to the backyard, now a paved parking lot that was completely full. Only after a customer drove off could the next one park. It took me thirty minutes after arriving to land a spot, which had given me plenty of time to chicken out, despite there being nothing to chicken out about, unless I was dumb enough—and I was not—to tell Brenda what I had done. I did not need her making some outrageous claim that buying pot was just the latest example of my supposed mid-life crisis, like she made about the tiny little sports coupe I bought a few months ago and sold soon thereafter because getting in and out of it hurt my back. Of course, I could counter such a claim by mentioning my suit; no one having a midlife crisis would have thought to wear one to buy pot. They would have worn ripped jeans, like most of the other people in line, and maybe a vintage 70s-band T-shirt, like a few of them. They probably would have worn a cap, too, in order to conceal their new bald spot.

My new bald spot is beginning to scorch in the blistering sun, so I would have worn my cap anyway, had I known I would be waiting outside. Waiting outside confused me at first, but now I understand it to be a security measure; with untold amounts of cash and drugs on hand, only a set num-ber of people are allowed inside the store at a time. Every once in a while, the door buzzes unlocked and a customer departs; after it snaps shut, the next customer is buzzed in. Cameras perched high on the wall are aimed at the door. When it is my turn to be buzzed in, I am tempted, in order to relax myself, and maybe to signal to the people who have joined the line and also look at me with suspicion and disdain that I am just a stoner like them, to smile at the camera and wave. But I am not dumb enough to do this either.

A few feet beyond the door I have entered is another door that leads to the showroom, and between both doors is a booth where a woman sits on a stool behind a glass partition.

I wave at her, which is dumb, and say I have come to buy cannabis, also dumb. She leans toward a microphone and this small enclosure fills with her one-word greeting: "Identification." I remove my driver's license from my wallet and slip it into the narrow slot beneath the partition. As she takes it, a man suddenly appears behind her. He looks angry as he begins to speak, and she looks angry when she responds, and while I am curious to know what they are saying I mostly wish they were not saying anything so I could get on with my purchase. Their exchange heats up and is supplemented with hand gestures. After a while the woman seems to realize that it is my driver's license with which she's making her point and slaps it onto a scanner. As my face materializes above her on a wall-mounted monitor, the man has one final say before leaving. The woman snatches up my license and shoves it into the slot. Then she reaches beneath her desk; the door to the showroom buzzes unlocked. I move toward it after scooping up my license, annoyed at having been made to bear witness to their altercation, another taint on my experience.

But what are mere taints considering the alternatives? It is not as if a squad car just came screeching around a corner, its spotlight blinding my crew and me as a command to *Freeze!* is barked from its loudspeaker, as had often happened. No one is shoving us against a wall or throwing us to the ground before conducting an aggressive body search complete with kicks and punches, demanding our weed and then, after finding or being directed to it, stuffing it into their pockets and telling us to get the hell out of there before they take our Black asses to jail. But sometimes they took our

Black asses to jail anyway, where we were locked up for as long as it took our fathers to come get us, unless we were on probation, in which case we would not be released to our fathers because this, for the foreseeable future, was our new home. "You want *this* to be your new home?" my father yelled at me once after picking me up. "Is *that* what you want? Because it's where you're headed, *boy*, if you don't get yourself together!" I did not want jail to be my new home and eventually got myself together, and now, with the legalization of marijuana, I often think of my friends whose pot selling, buying, and consumption led them to serious time behind bars, their lives ruined only for some politicians, some *suits*, to decide decades later that what was once a crime should be no more illegal than shopping at Tiffany.

Now I am upset. I try to will myself to leave the past in the past and embrace this moment as I make my way into the showroom. It helps that, unlike when I was outside, no one is paying me much attention. The customers are focused on the business at hand, meandering from counter to counter, peering inside and sometimes speaking with the hovering staff members, who are called, I learned on the store's website, "budtenders." I am pleased to see that some of the budtenders are my age, as are a couple of customers, but the name of the game remains youth. Youth and—what else to call it?—*joy*. Everyone seems to be in a very good mood. I would like to be in one too, which is why instead of beelining for the pickup window I see across the room, I opt to linger for a while. I stand at a counter and, like the people around me, stare at one of the buds. When it seems that I have stared at it long enough, I move to my right and stare at another one. I am staring at my third bud when from over the counter someone says, "Can I help you, sir?"

This is a first: being called "sir" by a drug dealer. A drug dealer, incidentally, or rather a *budtender*, who has borrowed Jerry Garcia's face. I thank him and say I am just looking.

"Well, if you're thinking of selecting the Lilac Diesel," he says, gesturing toward the bud before me, "you can't go wrong. It's one of our most refined hybrids, a bold engineered mix of the popular brands Forbidden Fruit, New York City Cherry Pie, Super Lemon Haze, and, of course, Citral Glue."

I nod thoughtfully, like I am considering the boldness of this mix and lean closer to the glass. When I look at the budtender again, he gives me more to consider. "It's noted for the stunning complexity," he says, "of its turpentine profile, and the subtle notes of citrus, sweet berries, earthy pine, and, a delight to all connoisseurs, but not as delightful, if you happen to be from a large city like me, the hints of gas." I nod some more, and now he tells me Lilac Diesel's percentages of THC and something called CBG, and then he praises Ethos Genetics, the Denver-based cannabis seed bank and creator of this "dynamic new strain" that, in addition to its aforementioned properties, "enhances creativity, focus, and drive."

All of that, I think, and no risk to my balls. "I'll take it," I say.

"Excellent choice," he responds. "Would you like buds or pre-rolls?"

Pre-rolls, I also learned from the website, are what we used to call joints. When I was a teenager, joints cost a dollar each. The budtender tells me these cost six dollars.

"*Six dollars?*" I repeat. "Those gas hints must be of high-octane premium."

"Actually," he says, "the price has been reduced, *just* for today."

A pot flash sale, another first. But it is not a first for me to have to resist a drug dealer's hard pitch, as I do after he tries to get me to pair the six pre-rolls I select with six pre-rolled Truffle Marmalade. "I've already ordered some gummies," I explain. He flinches, as if he is Bobby Flay and I just mentioned McNuggets. Or maybe he is trying to reconcile the idea of a Black, middle-aged suit getting high on candy, because that, as I initially suspected, is ridiculous. As he escorts me to the pickup window, I tell him the gummies are actually for my sons, and I hope, after he flinches again, this is my last dumb thing of the day.

The man at the pickup window is who I saw arguing with the woman in the booth earlier. He no longer looks angry, and the woman in the booth, when she buzzes me out a moment later, does not either. Whatever the reason for their confrontation, they seem to have gotten beyond it, which is more than I can say about the anxiety this excursion produced. Maybe I have just been too negatively conditioned to ever be able to buy drugs without at least being somewhat uptight. It is the same with buying liquor, the way my heart rate increases as I approach checkout counters, thanks to having approached liquor store checkout counters for five years, beginning when I was sixteen, with a fake ID. And of course, I still get anxious whenever I see the police while I'm driving, especially if they are in my rearview mirror, even though that anxiousness is accompanied by the near-certainty it's unwarranted. But what I wouldn't give to see a police officer in my rearview mirror now as I'm driving home! I would be tempted to intentionally get pulled over—run a stop sign, say, or fail to signal a lane change—and then, when the officer looks into my car to see my chewables and pre-rolls on the passenger seat, to laugh in his face. Society, the way I see it, owes me that too.

What I owe myself this very moment, I decide once I am home, is the experience of smoking pot with a complex turpentine profile. And notes of berries and pine. And hints of high-octane gas. Pot grown in labs by biochemists wearing goggles and white coats, high-end pot that stands no risks of actually being tree leaves, dirt, baking soda, tobacco, oregano or any of the other substances I had been scammed into buying from unscrupulous dealers; pot that is not laced with PCP or heroin like the kind that gave one of my friends a high from which he never fully returned; pot that while techni-cally pot is of such low quality it gives you a headache for two days. Above all, I owe myself pot that is legal, because what I am grappling with here, the way I'm seeing it now, is not a midlife crisis, but rather the lingering crisis of my youth.

This is what I am about to tell Brenda. She is standing over me, her hand still resting lightly on my shoulder, but I am no longer believing, as I did seconds ago when she woke me, that a budtender has borrowed her face. "Sleepy?" she asks.

I check my phone. Five thirty. She is home early. I sit up in one of the two Adirondack chairs on our back porch. "Yeah," I say, stretching my arms. "Thought I'd take a nap."

"You never take naps," she responds.

"True." I smirk and add, "Must be getting old!"

"Exactly," she says, smirking too, only not at me. I look to my right and see she is smirking at the saucer on the coffee table I used as an ashtray. It is holding the remaining nub of a Lilac Diesel pre-roll. The opened package with the other five pre-rolls is next to it, and next to that is the package of gummies.

That was dumb.

# THE BLESSING

I was asked to make this recording about my visit to Norfolk Prison yesterday, and here it is.[1] I don't know that I'll have much profound to say, but I will say it was probably one of the most profound experiences of my life, certainly as a writer.

I didn't know what to expect before I went, despite not being unfamiliar with prison. As I mentioned to the men,[2] I had spent some years as a juvenile delinquent and made my share of mistakes. I had been arrested for car theft in my teens,[3] resulting in my spending a couple of nights in the

---

1   It is two months later, and I've just listened to this recording for the first time.

2   I could not bring myself to refer to them as "inmates," my small way of affirming their humanity, but also, perhaps, my subconscious refusal, given the word's negative connotation, to state this basic fact.

3   Falsely. My twin brother stole the car and stripped it in our garage while I was at home sleeping. I awoke in my basement bedroom to see a steering wheel, a radio, four tires, two bucket seats, and two police officers, one of whom dangled a set of handcuffs. The other officer's set was already on my brother, who was in the police van.

local county jail.[4] And there were times when I had been arrested for marijuana possession or public intoxication, but typically on those occasions I was simply held overnight and released to my father.[5] My experience behind bars was minimal but real nonetheless, and so I thought it had prepared me for what I was about to experience. But it had not.

As we waited in the lobby,[6] I found myself becoming more and more anxious.[7] But then, once we entered the auditorium, I oddly felt somewhat at ease.[8] It was the anticipation, I think,

---

4   The time it took to make bail. Later, at our trial, despite my innocence but upon the advice of a public defender, I, like my brother, pleaded guilty. After sentencing us to three years of probation, and making clear that any violation of the law during that time would spell the end of our freedom, the judge rapped his gavel and said, "See you soon."

5   All of these arrests occurred prior to my being placed on probation for the car theft, which was why I never saw the judge again.

6   Myself and the five sponsors of my visit: two from the National Book Foundation, and three from Freedom Reads, a program founded by the acclaimed poet Reginald Dwayne Betts with the mission of installing easy-access libraries in prison housing units.

7   But this was nothing compared to the anxiety I felt once we were in the "hold," the area between the lobby and the prison's interior where we underwent a thorough search, including the inner waistlines of our pants, the bottoms of our shoeless feet, and in our ears and mouths. One of the organizers was initially denied entry because a small gap between the buttons of her blouse could possibly allow a glimpse of her bra, which could be problematic in ways I was unnerved to imagine. Before proceeding, she was provided a sweater.

8   For about ten seconds. By then I had taken in the crowd of roughly three hundred men, nearly all of whom were Black, which should not have shocked me, for I am well aware of the justice system's racial biases, but it did. Their boisterous chatter faded to murmurs as they watched us move toward the center of the empty stage. I had been asked in advance if I preferred to read from a podium or seated at a table. As a matter of habit, I had requested a podium, but none was there. Then I noticed that one had been placed on the floor, mere feet before the men occupying the front row. To the right of the podium were five folding chairs. A guard led us to them.

that was getting to me more than anything else, which is common for me prior to readings, and so I don't know if I could distinguish what I felt yesterday from what I generally go through.[9] But I was happy once the event was underway.

S_____ gave a remarkable introduction in which he talked about his own experience as someone who had been incarcerated, and I think that helped a great deal to put the men at ease and to be more welcoming toward me.[10] And so I began my reading after I had talked a little bit about my experiences leading up to becoming a writer, which I think the men appreciated.[11] They were very engaged with my reading, particularly when I read my essay called "The Second Act," which is about me stealing a bag of groceries and then returning them to the elderly woman I stole them from because I felt terribly guilty about it.[12] They were receptive to that, which was

---

9  Other than that, for the first time prior to a reading, my hands were visibly shaking, and I was drenched in sweat.

10  It also helped, per my request when I met S_____ in the lobby, that he not read my official author's bio. "Tell them I'm just a guy," I requested, "here to read my stuff." He smiled and nodded, obviously appreciative of my gesture. I received the same response from the audience when I rose and took the podium.

11  E.g., my dropping out of high school; teenage drug and alcohol abuse; the murder of my close friend, which precipitated the end of my delinquency, convincing me to earn my GED and to enroll in a community college, the message being that everyone has the capacity for redemption.

12  I was sixteen, intoxicated, and with a friend who was teaching me how to be a criminal. I, in contrast, was teaching my friend how to not be one by insisting we return the groceries, which we'd stolen from the trunk of the elderly woman's car after she'd carried one of the bags into her house. We were both poor students. Forty years later, I was in one prison as a guest author while he was in another serving a life sentence for murder.

great.[13] And then we had a Q&A, and I was impressed but not surprised by the intelligence of the questions. The men were genuinely interested in me as a writer and about how they might improve their own writing.[14]

I recently received a very nice note from S_____ thanking me for attending the event, and he said something that hadn't really occurred to me: the men were taking me through a "rite of passage" whereby they questioned my motives for wanting to be there, how sincere I was about being a part of this process, and whether or not they could in some way see me as being one of them, in some form of kinship. I did very much feel that I was being vetted at times, but I didn't feel it was antagonistic. I thought that it was appropriate that people want to make sure guests in their home are being respectful, thoughtful, and courteous about the process. So I didn't mind that at all. If fact, I appreciated it. The best part about the entire event was the Q&A. I could have gone on longer, but I knew that it was taking a little bit

---

13 They especially liked the essay's final scene: me standing alone on the elderly woman's porch, intending to ring the bell, leave the groceries and flee. When the door suddenly opened, I stammered that I'd witnessed her robbery and chased the thief, who unfortunately had escaped, I said, but I had gotten back her groceries. "God bless you," she said as I handed her the bags. "But I did not hear her," the essay concludes, "not for many years."

14 They were interested, too, in being published. "Do you know," one man asked, "if there are any literary magazines that focus on the topic of incarceration?" I did not know of any offhand, I responded, but I was sure that if they existed, they'd be easy to find. "Just google it," I said. There was an explosion of laughter, above which rose shouts that they did not have internet access. I laughed too, ignoring my rising body temperature, and the voice in my head telling me, "'Just a guy' would have known that."

longer than what we'd anticipated. But I had a really, really invigorating time.[15]

A curious thing happened after the reading. When I was being thanked by the group, shaking hands, and listening to them tell me a little about themselves, I felt like I knew many of them, that I'd grown up with them. Some even *looked* familiar. And I don't know if it was because the experience was taking me back to my youth, to the South Side of Chicago, and I was simply superimposing the images of people I'd grown up with onto these men.[16]

I've given many, many readings over the years, and I would certainly rank this experience right at the top. I don't think I've done anything as a writer sharing my work as important and as meaningful as what I experienced yesterday.

As I said, this was probably the best experience I've had as a writer, and even as a person. So I applaud the National Book Foundation and Reginald Dwayne Betts for founding

---

15  Near the end of the Q&A, I'd forgotten until now, as sweat dripped from my face, my shirt soaked through, I saw from the corner of my vision one of the men approaching me. He was holding a cup of water. "You're doing alright, brother," he whispered as he handed it to me. "You're doing alright." With that, I finally managed to relax.

16  These men had gotten bad breaks or squandered good ones, and what I now recall thinking was that their reasons for being there didn't matter in that moment, only that they seemed eager for whatever wisdom I had to impart, for the keys to a better life. They had self-selected, after all, in coming to my reading. There had been a snafu with the delivery of my books, so rather than have me sign their copies they handed me notepads, scraps of paper, the flyers advertising my appearance. These men, who had lost their way or had their way denied, were embracing me as an inspiration, as a role model, and I remember, now, how proud that made me feel.

this remarkable program, and for everyone who is involved in it. And I hope that the men with whom I spoke, and to whom I read, appreciated my presence as much as I appreciated theirs.

So thank you all, again, for this fantastic opportunity. I'm looking forward to the next one. I'm also looking forward to working with my colleagues in my department at my college who have been engaged in the prison system for quite some time.[17]

---

17  I ran into one of those colleagues a few hours ago. She mentioned hearing of my visit to Norfolk, which I had not thought of for some time, and because I am so deeply flawed in a way that I wish not to be what immediately came to mind was that I had been vetted and had my motives for being there questioned. I thought of my advice to the man to do a google search and the ensuing laughter, only now the laughter was not coming just from the inmates but from the members of the gang I had quit when I refused to use a gun; from the teenagers who had beaten me up and taken the pot I'd attempted to sell them; from the security guard who'd caught me shoplifting and from the police who'd caught me skipping school; from more people than I could recall who had witnessed my failed or half-hearted attempts to do the kinds of things that would have earned the respect of my delinquent peers, that would have had me be just one of the guys, as I had so desperately wanted. It was from the depths of this self-pity that I responded when my colleague asked how my visit had gone. "Not so well," I said. She looked bewildered. I *was* bewildered and surely looked it too as I listened to the recording and heard, in my own voice, the truth of what I had felt of the experience, how moving and positive it had been. It was as if, like the elderly woman I'd robbed, I had opened my front door to a stranger and, with immense gratitude, been returned what had been stolen.

## COMBAT MODE

You have lived here for eight years and now, for the first time, with only thirty minutes before the start of your open house, you see a roach. A big, fat, juicy one too, right in the foyer near the abstract painting that replaced your favorite family photo. The family photo was taken by the obstetrician who moments prior had delivered your second son; your radiant wife holds him, as you, radiant too, hold your bewildered toddler. A friend once described the photo as "Love Personified," and it is so very true, which makes it all the more upsetting that potential homebuyers might look at it and decide not to submit an offer, or to lowball one. And so in the weeks leading up to this moment, you removed the photo, along with two dozen others and all clues to your race. Now, out of nowhere, just as you and your wife are scrambling out the door, this fat-ass roach has appeared, as if, by virtue of its presence, to spill the beans.

This is not to say that the presence of one or more roaches means the presence of one or more Blacks, or vice versa. Nor is it to say that the presence of Black homeowners means the presence of neglect and disrepair. But these are persistent stereotypes that, with so much at stake, you cannot risk falling victim to. You have already closed on your new house, priced just shy of a million dollars, a stupefying amount for a Black boy from a housing project where, it must be said, there were roaches aplenty. They were in dresser drawers and kitchen cabinets and shoes and the boxes of Cap'n Crunch and grits and sometimes in your ears when you woke from dreaming about them. You wish you were dreaming about the one near your abstract painting because then you would not have to go into combat mode.

After shoving closed the door your wife just opened, you push off the heel of one of your shoes with the toe of the other. "What are you doing?" she asks. "What's wrong?"

"There's a roach."

"A what?"

"Roach."

"Where?"

"There."

Your wife looks up. "*Yikes*," she utters, recoiling.

"I have to kill it," you say.

"There's no time. We need to go."

"Are you *crazy*? We can't have white folks thinking we have *roaches*."

"We do, apparently."

"No, we don't. We have *a* roach. A scout, just casing the joint. I know how they operate."

You know how whites operate too. The ones in your neighborhood, for instance, with whom you have exchanged waves and occasionally small talk but never established the kind of relationships that would lead to an exchange of dinner invitations, will be among the first to enter your house when your Realtor opens its doors. You know they were among the thirteen hundred viewers the listing received within the first hour of it going live, as curious to see the renovations you had done as they were grateful that they were done, for unquestionably, when they saw your family move in, the first and only Black one in the neighborhood, they were nervous about what this could mean for their property value. *The renovations are stunning*, you can imagine them saying after their walk-through of your house, *but, of course, they have roaches.*

You kneel to get your shoe.

"There's *no time*," your wife says again.

"It'll just take a second," you respond. "I've got skills."

So does the roach; as you are rising with your weapon, it drops from the wall, requiring you to make an evasive maneuver whereby you fling yourself backward into the console holding the vase of fresh lilies your wife would not have purchased and spent so much time arranging had she known they would end up on the floor, scattered in a pool of water and broken ceramic. She heard but did not witness this catastrophe, however, for her own evasive maneuver entailed making a mad dash from the room while screaming bloody murder, as if the roach had landed upon her face or shoulder. That would have been ideal, you think. At least you would know where it is.

Shoe in hand, you hunt for it while your wife cleans up the mess. Five minutes is all you have allotted for your respective tasks, and even that is pushing your departure perilously close to when the open house begins. It would be a disaster to have gone through all the trouble of scrubbing your house of your racial identity only to have it revealed by your actual bodies. It's bad enough that ever since the Realtor put the "For Sale" sign on your lawn two weeks ago, there has been an increase of traffic in front of your house, all day and evening cars creeping by and sometimes pausing to idle as their occupants take in your property but not your skin color because you were peering at them through a part in the blinds. Your wife said you were taking things too far, once again crossing the gulf between caution and lunacy. You begged to differ. If this house does not sell quickly at or above market value, you reminded her, you will, as a result of juggling two mortgages, be up shit's creek.

You were nearly up it a few years ago when you applied for a home equity loan to put toward your oldest son's college tuition. The loan was declined, thanks to the appraiser undervaluing your house by 30 percent. You were furious but not surprised, considering that when you had answered the door for the appraiser, he asked to see the owner. As if you were, what, the doorman? The goddamn butler? As if, as you escorted him through the house, showing him the new addition and pointing out other upgrades, you were not speaking a familiar language because he was not taking notes. For the entire time he was there, his clipboard hung at his side, as useless a thing as the lips he'd been given to smile.

You appealed the appraisal and won. But it had taken a lot of time and effort, hours you did not have to spare of compiling comps and producing improvement receipts. It had taken some luck too; the next appraiser the bank sent was Black and assumed your ownership rather than servitude and whose clipboard and smile-able lips were put to frequent use. And it had nearly taken some deception; you seriously considered having two white friends pretend to be you and your wife. You got that idea from a recent news report about a Black couple who, after also having an appraisal come back far below market value, removed all their family photos and had white friends pretend to be them for another appraisal, which ended up being accurate. So you probably should have done that. And this time, instead of replacing your favorite family photo with abstract art, you probably should have replaced it with the favorite family photo of your white friends. But that would have been difficult to explain to your white Realtor, who, as your white friends did when you floated this idea, would have thought you were a lunatic.

"I see that big motherfucker!" you yell, pointing at the roach with your shoe.

Your wife, who has just come out of the kitchen holding a new vase with the lilies, stands at your side. "How did it get *up there*?" she asks.

She is referring to the ceiling, and also, figuratively, to her lack of experience.

"Roaches," you explain, "can bend time and space."

"This isn't a joking matter."

You rest your case.

"Maybe," she continues, "it'll stay there and no one will notice it."

"It won't."

On cue, the roach darts out of the corner. You are tempted to throw your shoe at it but fear the mark it and, if you are successful, the roach could leave on the ceiling. "Get the broom," you say. "I'll keep an eye on it."

"Okay," she says, hurrying to the kitchen, "but it won't reach." At the moment, this is true. You are in the open-concept dining and living room where the angled ceiling is fourteen feet at its apex. But the roach is zigzagging toward the ceiling's lower end of eight feet. It doesn't make it, though. By the time your wife returns with the broom, it has paused midway, near the fan. You both watch it descend the fan's extension pole. When it crawls along the edge of one of the blades, its bloated body is almost completely camouflaged by the walnut finish. If you hadn't been watching it, you wouldn't know it was there.

Your wife hands you the broom and then looks at her watch. "The open house starts in ten minutes."

"Okay, okay," you respond, and then you tell her, based on the expertise that was forced upon you, what the roach is doing. "It's taking in the situation, planning its next move. Just give it a moment."

After giving it a moment, your wife snatches the broom from you and returns it to the kitchen. She comes back and goes directly to the door. "Let's *go*," she demands.

You look from the roach to her and back to the roach, and then you look from the roach to the coffee table, on which sits the fan's remote. The remote has six speeds, the highest three of which you've only used once. The problem is the fan's five hundred RPMs motor and five-foot blade span, which, when you purchased it from the industrial fan store, you thought would be necessary to create a nice breeze in this large space. But the nice breeze you hoped for can be achieved at the fan's lowest setting. Its highest setting produces a cyclone.

"Do *not*," your wife says, right before you pick up the remote, "even think about it." Rather, she should have said, "*Do* think this through," for that big fat-ass roach will soon be airborne again, this time at a velocity impossible to evade should the great odds against it heading directly at either of you be overcome. Your wife *has* thought this through, evidently, because when you press the remote's highest setting, she rushes outside to the driveway, where you will join her after the roach has been propelled against a wall before landing on the floor, its ability to undermine your house sale ending with three whacks of your shoe.

A moment later, as you run down the porch steps, a car pulls into your driveway and stops alongside you and your wife. It is only your Realtor, thank goodness. But the street, you notice, is already lined with a dozen cars of prospective buyers, all eager to get a good look at your house and now having gotten a good look at the two Black people who fled it. It is likely that among these prospects are the two house hunters who will submit offers within the hour. Both offers will be well above asking price. You will accept the highest one, needless to say, along with your belief that, had only your departure not been delayed, you would have gotten more.

# THIS MATH

We arrive with time to spare, despite the five taxi
drivers who refused to bring us. I had hoped that, in
this day and age, such bias against Harlem was behind us, or
at least that drivers had learned to discern which potential
fares might lure them into trouble. But in case that bias remained, Dorian, at my insistence, along with a brand-new
polo shirt, is wearing matching socks. I instructed Adrian to
wear his T-shirt with his alma mater's initials emblazoned on
the front. Brenda is disarming in a pink sundress, and I, whenever a taxi approached, slipped on my readers. Unfortunately,
our portrait of Black wholesomeness assured us only of getting
drivers' attention, not their services. I give the driver who ac-
cepted us a large tip that I regret even before we exit the taxi.
All he has done, after all, is his job.

I will acknowledge, however, that this street looks a little
sketchy. A block before we pulled to the curb, I had been taking note of a sprawling housing project, certain that at any
moment, due to the constant talk of Harlem's gentrification,
there would be evidence of an economic upturn, culminating
with us disembarking before a Starbucks and an Au Bon

Pain. Instead, we were about to disembark before a fried chicken joint and a man selling watermelons. The fried chicken joint is gated, bolted, and covered in graffiti, as are a number of other defunct businesses surrounding it. Maybe our driver, who has a thick Tunisian accent—I had, by way of small talk, which seemed expected of me since I was in the passenger's seat, inquired of his origins—misunderstood the address I provided. I am not one of those people who assume someone with a thick accent has difficulty understanding English, but I am one of those people who mumble. Half the time my own family has no idea what I'm saying. "Are . . . you . . . sure," I asked in my best enunciation, "we . . . are . . . at . . . the . . . correct . . . place?"

"I . . . am . . . sure." This he'd said with an eye roll.

I glanced over my shoulder at Brenda; she'd made the reservations. "Did you give me the right address?" I asked. When she said she had, I looked back at the driver, who was looking in his side-view mirror, as if he thought my skepticism was feigned and a part of our scam, a delay tactic to get the robbers in position. But if a scam was at play, it occurred to me, it had been perpetrated by whomever sold us our fake tickets.

And we are not alone. As soon as our taxi pulls away, another takes its place, from which an elderly white couple emerges holding tickets like ours. "Two more dupes," I whisper to Brenda and the boys, but they are gone; I turn to see them several feet behind me entering an open business I somehow missed. I hurry after them, holding the door for the trailing couple when I reach it.

A man in his mid- to late forties, wearing a T-shirt and a cap that say "Harlem," sits at a desk staring at a computer. Before him are a dozen occupied folding chairs. Brenda and the boys are standing in the rear with five other people. I join them before glancing at my phone's clock; the walking tour begins in ten minutes. Until then, it appears our guide will contemplate his computer, so I pass the time contemplating the photographs of famous Harlemites circling the room: W. E. B. Du Bois, Marcus Garvey, Muhammad Ali, James Baldwin, Zora Neale Hurston, and, of course, Malcolm X. There is also one of former president Barack Obama, for which, I feel, the curator can be forgiven; I have long believed Obama is Malcolm reincarnated, updated to suit the times.

Three more people arrive. Because I am hardwired to do this math, our count is now eight whites, two Asians, three Others, and ten Blacks—eleven including the guide. I assume the guide is doing this math too as he finally looks up and scans the room, a finger bobbing at each of our heads, the final tally of which will likely dictate the substance and style of his narration. A Blacks-only tour, like all Blacks-only everything, would have its own distinct flavor. That would have been especially true of an all-Black tour of an all-Black Harlem.

Brenda and I got a taste of what that might have been like thirty-five years ago when, while on vacation in Times Square, as we are this week, we came to Harlem to visit my cousin. He had turned up here in a halfway house after vanishing from Chicago without a trace a decade prior, leading everyone to conclude he was dead, a high probability based on his lifestyle. "Things had gotten too hot," he told Brenda and me. "Too much crime and violence, too many gangs." Harlem, from what I had heard, seemed a poor choice of refuge, but he insisted that was not true. Nowhere in the world, he said, was there a more welcoming, supportive community. Three hours later, after we'd finished meandering through Harlem's residential streets, we had reason to agree. Everyone we had encountered was warm and friendly, and one man, sensing our foreignness, asked if we needed a place to stay. My math put these encounters at 90 percent Black; where, I wonder, are all those people now? Had they, like my cousin, been forced out due to the soaring cost of housing, replaced by white folks with money? During an all-Black tour, I am certain the scourge of gentrification would be a hot topic. I assume it would be bad for business to mention it in mixed company.

The head and racial count taken, the guide rises, introduces himself, and asks us to state where we're from. A young couple kicks things off by saying they are newlyweds on honeymoon from Ghana, which is met with applause. Next, someone says Amsterdam, followed by San Diego, Miami, and New Jersey. Then a middle-aged Black man near me puffs himself up and says "Detroit" with an elongated "e," like there are two of them. This is also applauded. When it's my family's turn, I decide to give *us* a distinct flavor by saying "Chiraq," but Brenda beats me to the punch. "Hingham!" she says. This is met with raised eyebrows. "It's a small coastal town," she explains, "twenty miles south of Boston." There is no applause.

When every place of origin has been declared, the guide says, "This is why I love my job. I get to meet people from all over the world." He grins and adds, "Now, let me introduce you to the *best* place of all!"

Once we are outside walking, I lean toward Brenda and quietly tell her, "You should have said Chiraq."

"Iraq?"

"*Chi*raq. That's what I would have said."

She snorts. "It would have been your first time."

"I've said Chiraq before."

"Well, I've never heard you."

"That doesn't mean I haven't said it."

"Okay, *Chiraq*." This she'd said with air quotes.

"Listen, everyone," the guide begins. He has stopped and is facing the group, beckoning us in tight. "All those buildings you see there," he says, as he points across the street, "are a housing project. It's where I was born and raised. My mama was too. She still lives there, so you might get to meet her, because that's our first stop." Brenda and I exchange a look, and I wonder if, like me, she is thinking of Johannesburg.

We were there for one night in 1996, a layover on our way from Harare, Zimbabwe, to Durban, South Africa. In need of a break from her dissertation fieldwork, we'd spontaneously decided on a credit-card-funded road trip. While checking into the hotel, the clerk mentioned some things we could do during our brief stay, including taking a bus tour of Soweto. "Do you know it?" he asked. We knew Soweto: the township founded in 1931 during the Apartheid government's resettlement act in order to remove Blacks from the city center; the township with the iconic images of colorful wall-to-wall shanties with roofs of sheet metal; the township where, in 1976, riots made international news and left dozens of Blacks dead after the government's decree that students had to be taught in Afrikaans instead of Zulu; the township that Brenda's Zimbabwean relatives and our travel books warned us to avoid, for its dangers were internationally known too. And yet we'd been eager to see it. Now here was our chance to do so in the safety of a guided tour. The next morning, we bought two tickets we could not bring ourselves to use after seeing the queue for the bus, which was comprised entirely of whites, cameras dangling from their sunburned necks, as if they'd just completed one safari and were embarking on another. The unease I felt then is the unease I feel now.

But our guide, having detected my unease, mistakes it for fear. "Don't worry, everyone," he says, while looking directly at me. "No one will get mugged or robbed." He winks. Dee-troit chuckles.

We have crossed the street and are standing in the heart of the project's courtyard. To our right is a basketball court with a game being cheered by thirty or so spectators. To our left are swings, seesaws, and monkey bars where kids are hard at play, women watching them from nearby benches. There are several other benches, some with teenagers and some with seniors. All around us people are going about their midday business. None of them pays us any attention, but we, per our guide's instructions, pay attention to them. "The projects get a bad rap," he says, "but as you can see, these are just normal folk, doing normal things. Let's just appreciate this for a minute." When the minute of appreciation passes, he directs our attention toward the top of one of the buildings. "Do you see that window, the one with the green curtains? That's where I was born. My mama has lived there her whole life. I don't know if she's home right now, but in case she is, let's wave."

We wave at his mother's window. Some of the tourists take pictures of it, which leads to picture taking of the playing children, the teenagers and seniors on benches, and the people going about their business. When a picture is taken of the basketball players, the guide says to be sure to get one of the kid in the red shirt. "Straight A student," he says, "a future leader of his people, like these young men here." He gestures toward Adrian and Dorian. "Mr. and Mrs. Coastal Town have done an outstanding job raising them; you know how I know?" He moves close to Adrian and puts his arm around his shoulders. "Because this brother is proudly wearing his BSU shirt, which, for those of you who don't know, stands for Black Student Union."

*Just let it go, Adrian,* I think, *just let it go . . .*

"Actually," Adrian begins, "the BSU stands for Bridgewater State University."

"Say what now?"

"Bridgewater State University."

The guide looks from Adrian to Brenda and me, and then beyond us, his confused expression giving way to one of delight. He parts the group to embrace the petite, gray-haired woman who has joined us. "Everyone," he says, "say hello to my mama!"

We do, and then she smiles warmly and asks, "Is my baby taking good care of y'all?"

"Now you *know* I am, Mama," he responds, smiling too. "We're about to head to the African market, but first I wanted to let everyone see how nice it is here."

"It certainly is," she confirms. "I've lived here *all* my life and don't intend to leave! If they ever tear this place down, y'all will find me right here, somewhere beneath the rubble."

She and her son laugh, and as everyone joins in my unease gives way to an ache for my own mother. She would have made an equally effective hostess, I think, had a tour group appeared on our project's front lawn. After the guide hugs his mother once more, she thanks us for visiting before continuing toward her building. "This way," the guide says, heading in the opposite direction. We fall in step behind him, all except for Dee-troit, who joins him at his side.

This is common: a member of a tour group cozying up to the guide for a private conversation, getting more bang for their buck if the conversation is tour-related, or, if it's not, brownnosing because it's what they do. I don't know if Dee-troit is brownnosing, but I would be following up on his mother's mention of the projects' possible demolition, a subtle reference to gentrification that the African market seems to embody. I believe it is the same one my cousin brought Brenda and me to. There are only two rows of merchandise and, other than our tour group, no customers, but thirty-five years ago the market spanned a city block. And judging from some of the price tags on the merchandise I see now, it was considerably less expensive. For a steal I had bought a mahogany walking cane with a gold-plated handle, an odd purchase for sure, but I had been swept up by the market's festive atmosphere and its pulsating Afro-centrism, as well as by the proprietor's charm and persistence. These proprietors greet us warmly, but they do not pitch their goods. They seem indifferent, even, to our presence. No one buys anything. After just a few minutes, the tour resumes.

So too does Dee-troit's brownnosing; I am fairly certain now this is what he's doing. Over the next hour, I become convinced of it. In between every stop, after the guide has explained a site's historical and cultural significance, after photos have been taken and questions asked and answered, he barely has a chance to lead us away before Dee-troit cozies up to him and begins again. Their conversations pause only whenever passersby near their orbit, whom the guide never fails to greet with an enthusiasm he takes up a notch if they're Black. And then, after the passerby has moved on, the guide makes the point to our group that Harlemites are welcoming and hospitable. It is the same point my cousin seemed bent on making, the difference being that he had more Blacks with which to make it. At least a quarter of everyone I've seen since we arrived are white, a percentage that sharply increases when we enter the residential streets lined with beautifully restored brownstones.

Our guide stops at one now. "*This* property," he says, "belonged to the Lady herself, Maya Angelou." She purchased it in 2002, he tells us, for a half-million dollars. In 2016, two years after her death, it sold for $4.5 million. Our mouths still agape, he gathers us on the stairs for a group picture. I wonder if the current homeowners mind this, or if they had understood it would come with the territory. The house belonged to the Lady, after all, and the Lady belonged to the community, which in turn, at least for the time being, belongs to people who look like her. And who knows? Maybe the current owners look like her as well. I would like to believe they do.

A few houses down, there's a white woman sitting on the porch steps, a little girl at her side, eating a Popsicle. As we reach them, our guide says hello with his characteristic zeal, and the woman politely responds while looking our group over. "Is this some kind of tour?" she asks. I am perplexed by the question (we are obviously some kind of tour), but I am even more perplexed that she appears confused after the guide says yes, like she cannot conceive of a tour's purpose, like she has no understanding of where she is. If she has perplexed the guide as well, he does not let on. He just offers her his card.

But she's forced his hand; either that or by sheer coincidence this is the part of the tour, among the refurbished multimillion-dollar brownstones, where he always mentions gentrification. We have reached an intersection, its "Do Not Walk" sign flashing overhead, and he's telling us that during the last decade, Harlem's Black population decreased by ten thousand people. "Its white population," he adds, "during the same period, increased by twenty thousand." He lets these numbers hang in the air for a moment, a dramatic pause before he rails against gentrification, a part of me hopes, only it turns out to be a dramatic stop. He's faced the street, indicating he'll say no more on the subject, which, considering our math, is not perplexing in the least. What is perplexing, however, is that I am only now realizing his rail against gentrification is the substance and style of the tour itself, an affirmation less of a place than of the people who, like him and his mother, seemed determined to keep it. "Yes, We Can," he's been proclaiming all along, or, for those of us who know, "By any means necessary."

The light turns green. When the guide steps forward, I maneuver past Dee-troit and fall in step with him. "I just wanted to say," I begin, "how much I'm enjoying the tour."

"Thank you, brother. I appreciate that."

"It's been outstanding in every way."

"Thank you."

"And it was really nice to meet your mother."

Chuckling, he says, "She's something else."

"I got the feeling," I say, chuckling too, and then lowering my voice, "just between us, that some people were uneasy about going to the projects."

He looks at me slyly and asks, "How about you?"

I consider saying yes, a little, and then mentioning the Soweto tour, but instead I offer an affirmation of my own. "It was my favorite part," I say. "Brought back some good memories."

"How so?"

"I was born in the projects too."

"*Really*?" he says. "Whereabouts?"

"Chicago," I say, "or, as I like to call it, *Chiraq*."

Nodding, he offers me his fist. I bump it with mine.

We are across the street now, standing before another brownstone. "Gather around, everyone," he says. A semicircle forms before him. As he begins to talk, I blend back into the group, positioning myself between the boys and Brenda.

Brenda takes my hand. She leans toward me and whispers, "That looked to be some pretty impressive brownnosing."

"It's what I do."

This I'd said while smiling.

But no one in my family is smiling an hour after the tour has ended. We have spent this time scurrying from intersection to intersection, seeking ones with high traffic flow in hopes of increasing our odds of spotting a taxi. We remain in one place when Brenda downloads an app that is supposed to be able to deliver a taxi to us. None of the first three she summons materializes. By the time the fourth one does, now an hour and a half after the tour's end, I'm frustrated enough to tip the driver poorly. But I know I won't. After all, it's not his fault we've had to wait so long. He's just doing his job.

# THE SLIP

I was robing for commencement when two Black colleagues informed me of my slip. "You were *working* it," one said, before the other added: "Don't work it *too* hard, though, or you'll scare the white folks." I had no idea what they were talking about, but scaring the white folks, unless by intention, was something I preferred to avoid. I asked what I had done, causing them to break into laughter that abruptly ceased when they realized I was not joking. With expressions of curiosity and concern, they recounted seeing me a short while earlier, as I made my way across campus, doing the gangster walk.

Not to be confused, I should stress, with "the gangsta walk," a dance made popular by the Memphis-based band G-Style in the 1990s. Apparently, I had been walking like the actual gangster I had once been—not a good one, certainly, but I had mastered the look of a good one in motion. Or rather in *slow* motion, my pace being that of a ninety-year-old with a leg wound. I also did this thing where I dipped one swaying shoulder slightly lower than the other and fanned the air behind me with my cupped hands, unless they were holding, as they often were back then, a forty-ounce and a joint. "The only thing I was missing," I said, to my colleagues, "was a forty-ounce and a joint!" This time we all laughed, but in truth, I was mortified. I think they were too.

I resumed robing, already beginning to fret over how my body, unbeknownst to my brain, had spoken in the manner I had trained it as a teen, telling onlookers, "Do *not* mess with me" and "I'm a *killer*" and "There's a *bullet in my thigh*." But it is not often these days that my body needs to say such things. In fact, the only real occasion is when my class ends at 9:45 PM and, to reach the underground parking garage in the Boston Common, I must, regrettably, enter the Boston Common. The Boston Common is not safe at 9:45 PM. It is not safe at many other times either. If faculty must enter it, our campus police recommends that we use their escort service. I never have, though, because that would be at odds with my body when it tells onlookers, "I'm cool."

On a gangster-walk scale of one to ten, "cool" would be a two. Two is my normal. Based on my colleagues' reaction, I must have crept up to three, maybe four. Four is what I reserve for the Boston Common. I never go above four unless I am visiting my old neighborhood on the South Side of Chicago, in which case, having largely aged out of being seen as a threat by threatening people, a six is sufficient. But there was that time I visited a few years ago when my twin brother coaxed me into going with him to a liquor store, and just to play it safe (it was night), I ratcheted it up to eight. My brother was impressed. I still had it, he said.

And now, I feared, it had me. How often, I wondered, had

I unknowingly exceeded a level two? Could it be that as I advanced into middle age, my body, as a precursor to my mind, was regressing to an earlier time and place? Was I destined to do a high-level gangster walk with a walker? I was picturing myself in a nursing home, scaring the elderly white folks, when an announcement came over the intercom: procession was about to begin. I put on my mortarboard, tilting it just so, and then joined the other faculty assembling by the door, making sure to be in front to secure the best seat. Soon thereafter, as the band started to play, we were ushered into the auditorium. The crowd rose and applauded at the sight of us, and I willed my body, like never before, to speak only of my coolness as I moved down the aisle. Was this my life now? I wondered. Being extra careful, figuratively, and in due course, literally, not to slip?

I tried to stop thinking about it in order to enjoy myself. Commencement, in my opinion, one shared by very few of my colleagues, was the best part of being an academic. The ceremonies were endless, my colleagues complained, and more often than not the speeches were boring, trite, and clichéd. All of this was true. And yet I loved every minute of it, perhaps only in a way a Black high school dropout from the ghetto could, for I knew firsthand the transformative power of education. Had I not abandoned the streets and enrolled at a community college, I, like so many of my family and friends, would have gangster-walked to prison or an early grave. It was unlikely that any of the few Black students at the private college where I now worked were high school dropouts from the ghetto, but it was a good bet that their journey to this point had been more difficult than their white peers'. That was why my enjoyment of commencement increased when I saw Black students all decked out in their regalia, faces beaming as they mounted the stage and waited for their names to be called, and then, once they were, to proudly march forward, pausing, after a few steps, in the case of the young man there now, to do the crip walk.

Which *was* to be confused with the gangbangers' dance of that name, for it was a gangbanger, Robert "Sugar Bear" Jackson, who, in Compton, California, during the 1970s, had started it. But I assumed the student was doing the dance's pop-culture version, the one being performed by all manner of people the world over, and even once, in 2006, on PBS by a Teletubby. I had even attempted it myself a number of times and might have succeeded but for my patellar tendonitis. Unfortunately for me, the dance involves a series of intricate steps, executed at the speed and rhythm of the dancer's choosing, with slow and smooth being the choice of the student onstage as he inched toward the diploma in the president's hands. It was the student's own hands that suddenly brought into question which version of the dance he was doing; his index fingers and thumbs appeared to be formed into a C, the Crips' gang sign. It was possible, it occurred to me, that the young man was saying more than that he was ecstatic. He could have been saying, "I'm a killer." If that were the case, it would have been no truer of him, I was certain, than of me.

But there had been a time when crip walking, with or without the hand gesture, would have spoken truthfully of

the performer's propensity to kill, since the dance was decidedly limited to Crips, and Crips were decidedly killers. Its
members crip-walked at parties to show their gang affilia-
tion, but they also were known to do it at murder scenes, a
gruesome ritual whereby the dancers spelled "CRIP" with
their feet near the deceased victim, who more often than not
was a member of the Bloods, a rival gang. But inevitably, the
dance seeped into the broader Black culture, from which it
inevitably seeped into broader American culture, and then,
inevitably, into world culture. The seep became a gush in
2001 after the gangster rapper Dub-C's rendition of it at the
Up in Smoke hip-hop tour and later in his music videos.
MTV, aware of the dance's origins, refused to air his or anyone's videos that contained it. Many elementary and high
school administrators, also aware of this origin, added it to
their lists of prohibitions.

The 2012 Olympic organizers might have also added it
to their list of prohibitions, had they known that Compton
native Serena Williams would crip-walk on Wimbledon's
Centre Court after defeating Maria Sharapova for the
Olympic gold medal. Serena did not flash the gang sign, of
course, but even if she had, she was no killer either. And yet
for all the criticism she received, one would have thought
Sharapova had bled out near the net, the handle of Serena's
racket protruding from her chest. "Yup, that's what we need
representing America," one critic said, "a gold medalist who,
upon winning, glorifies hardened criminals who murder
each other—and innocent Americans—for sport." Another
critic called her "immature and classless."

Serena, regretful, it seemed, for the manner of her celebration, appeared to sense the coming heat during her post-victory press conference and sought to avert it. "Actually, there is a name," she responded, when reporters asked what the dance was called. "But I don't know if . . . it's inappropriate. It's just a dance we do in California." Finding it quite appropriate, however, was Snoop Dogg, also a Compton native, who, eight years later, would crip-walk during the 2020 Super Bowl LVI Halftime Show and receive no heat for it. "Shout out to Serena Williams," Snoop tweeted. "C walking at the Olympics Cpt style hahahahah! Go girl." For another of Serena's other supporters, a shout-out came in the form of a reasoned defense. "She didn't do it on purpose," she said. "It was a moment of unbridled joy. She pumped her fist, jumped up and down, looked into the crowd, then did her ill-timed dance."

When my colleagues had informed me of my ill-timed gangster walk, I had assumed it was an unbridled response to some threatening incident buried deep in my subconscious, but as I watched the student crip-walk, it occurred to me that wasn't the case. My body, on its own accord, as I was sure had been the case with Serena's, and very likely the student's too, was simply performing an act of homage, paying respects to a place where the flames of violence and hardship often consume lives, yes, but more often than not, as the writer Albert Murray observed, those flames forge lives into steel.

The student at last reached the president and received his diploma. He waved it at the applauding crowd before exiting the stage. The next student was called, and the next, and the next. I cheered each one, but a little less robustly, I admit, near the end. The ceremony lasted a new record of four hours. I was relieved and grateful for it to be over. My bad knee, bent for so long, had begun to throb. As my row was directed to process, my body, this time with my brain's full awareness, spoke to all who saw me limping down the aisle. "I'm not trying to scare the white folks," it said. "I'm just getting old."

## ON GETTING ALONG

The dinner's laughter and frivolity are punctuated by praise for my mixology and the coffee-marinated mutton chops with balsamic reduction that Brenda, an amateur chef, prepared to perfection, until someone mentions his plans for Sunday, followed by two others mentioning theirs, which results in a kind of roll call—*apple picking . . . antiquing . . . grading papers*—and when it is my turn, I make the mistake, brought on, no doubt, by an imprudent third Manhattan, of saying, "Watching football." The room falls silent. I reach for my glass, discover it is empty, and settle for eating the brandied cherry before scanning my friend's faces, all eight of which, incidentally, are white. "Needless to say," I continue, having gathered my bearings, "I will, for *every* game, be wearing my Kaepernick jersey."

And so begins another roll call.

"Wearing Kaepernick's jersey is *not* enough."

"Definitely not."

"Unless you're making this about you, Jerald."

"It's not about *you*."

"It's about Black people."

"I am," I say, "Black people."

"The Black *masses*."

"Brenda and I, together, qualify as masses."

"Don't tell us you're watching football too, Brenda?"

"No," Brenda says, "I don't like football."

"Neither do I, but *if* I did, I'd boycott it."

"For *Kap*!"

"Take a knee for him, Jerald."

"Really, you should."

"You simply *must*."

"I simply *must*," I say, "have more of this mutton." I poke a chunk of it into my mouth and chew with great deliberation while plotting my next move. I could just say I'll boycott the games, except that I do not like the idea of appearing susceptible to shaming. But if I stand my ground, it will be at the risk of ruining the evening's good cheer and possibly, should things get out of hand, some friendships. There are several hotheads among us, after all, with my head being the hottest.

I look from my friends' disappointed expressions toward the kitchen where, on the counter, the bottles of rye and vermouth, having set a fine example, must wonder why can't we all just get along. It is essentially the question being asked by Colin Kaepernick, as Rodney King asked long before him, as I asked long before Rodney King while in the back of a squad car. The officer to whom I put the question was sitting next to me with his revolver pressed against my gut; his partner was in the parking lot, beating my friend with a baton. My friend and I were sixteen and had skipped school to get high, a lack of judgment I compounded by insulting the mother of the officer at my side. Now he was about to make good on his threat to kill me, unless, as I later assumed must have been the case, he was moved by my tears and pleas for mercy.

I also assumed that killing me would not have led to his prosecution. I had made a play for his weapon, he would have claimed, his partner would have agreed, and my death, like those of countless Blacks at the hands of police, would have gone unrecorded by history, since it would have gone unrecorded by video. As I consider possible responses to my dinner guests, I think of saying that if and when police brutality comes to an end, it will not be because Colin Kaepernick kneeled during the national anthem. It will be because Philippe Kahn invented the camera phone.

But unlike Philippe Kahn, Colin Kaepernick is in the eyes of many a hero. Here is a man, after all, who as a matter of deep conviction refuses "to look the other way," as he explained, while there are "bodies in the street and people getting paid leave and getting away with murder." I appreciate his conviction, as I appreciate how it has not compelled him to quit the game we both love. It will not even compel him to quit it after he compares the NFL's Black players to slaves in three years, a time that will find my friendships with my dinner guests still intact. But first we have to survive the night.

"I cannot take a knee for Kaepernick," I say, after swallowing my mutton, "because of my father." His image suddenly appears before me, as it often does whenever I think of or mention him. And the image is usually the same: he is in our living room reclined on one of the two La-Z-Boys, wearing dress slacks and a white button-down, his work clothes transformed into his leisure clothes by forgoing the blazer and tie. In most of my memories of him, it is the weekend, so he is not at the Lighthouse for the Blind, where he taught Braille and counseled young people who had lost their sight.

"My father lost his sight," I say, "as I believe most of you know, after accidentally falling and hitting his head when he was twelve." It was a traumatic experience, I continue, one he felt he might not have emotionally survived but for sports. They provided him with what at the time he needed most: examples of perseverance, determination, and mental and physical strength. "They gave him the will *to try*," I add. "And much later, when his and my relationship was strained and on the verge of severing, sports gave him the means to try to heal that too." I explain how my father and I clashed often, especially during my teenage years, but we were in agreement when it came to the beauty of sports. He liked baseball and hockey, whereas I preferred hoops, but we shared a passion for football. "Without fail," I say, "in a kind of truce, we would gather in the living room on Sunday as kickoff neared, him on one recliner, me on the other."

The television would be muted, I tell my friends, because the announcers did not provide much descriptive detail, certainly not the kind that brought the action alive for the visually impaired. For that, my father relied on radio broadcasters, but sometimes, I say, he relied on me. "To this day, I sometimes watch the games on mute and provide play-by-play for my father, as if he were still alive, as if he were *with* me. So I cannot," I conclude, "as I hope you now understand,

take a knee for Kaepernick, because to do so, you see, would
be to take a knee against the man whose spirit, every Sunday, sits at my side."

The room falls silent again. This time Brenda breaks it.
"Dessert, anyone?" she asks, rising. She enters the kitchen at
the start of the next roll call.

"Thank you, Jerald, for sharing that story."

"Yes, thank you."

"*So* moving."

"Just precious."

"I'm sorry, Jerald, if I offended you."

"Me too."

"So am I."

"Sincere apologies."

"We didn't know."

"You should have told us."

"Brenda, why didn't Jerald tell us?"

Brenda, who has just returned carrying a large tray of
dessert, responds, "Flambéed vanilla-poached pears!" She
sets the tray on the table to cheers. Someone inquires about
the recipe; someone else asks how it is made; dinner plates
are hastily cleared, and the delicacy is served. As we have
our first bites, compliments intermingle with groans of
pleasure. In short order, frivolity and laughter ebb back into
the conversations, none of which includes the NFL or
Kaepernick. One would not have known they were ever
mentioned until the evening's final roll call when, as we say
our goodbyes at the door, everyone tells me to enjoy the
games.

"That meal," I say to Brenda, once we are alone, "could quite possibly have been your finest."

"I wish I could say the same," she replies, "about what you served."

"What do you mean?"

"Wearing your Kaepernick jersey before every game?"

"I would not rule it out," I insist, "if I owned one."

"Maybe I'll buy you a couple," she says. "One for you, and one for your *father's spirit*."

He would have appreciated that detail, I think, since we shared a sense of humor, as opposed to, say, the same room during the games. My brothers and I watched them on the television in the basement. Our father listened to them on the living room radio. It *is* true, however, that he and I often clashed when I was a teenager, a period of my life, particularly as it pertains to our relationship, I would do over if I could.

On Sunday, right before kickoff, in a fantasy I'm having of such a do-over, my father is sitting with me on my couch. We both have on Kaepernick jerseys, his snug over his white button-down. The TV is muted. The color guard is marching onto the field, I tell my father, followed by a woman with a microphone. The crowd and the players stand at attention, including Kaepernick, who starts to wind past his teammates until he is in clear view of a camera. As the national anthem begins, he places not *one* hand on his heart, but *two*. The crowd, watching him on the jumbotron, breaks into applause, for this gesture, he explained beforehand, is how he honors the good cops who protect Black lives in the face of the bad ones who harm them, resulting, indirectly, in the issue of police brutality being brought to the fore. It's a shrewd move on Kaepernick's part, elegant in its cunning and execution. And in this way, my father and I agree, the question of us all getting along is answered.

## MINSTREL I

These *Soul Train* videos got me dancing like I'm a teenager back in the hood throwing down for some honeys, and not fifty-eight and alone in my suburban den. Before long, I've worked up a sweat and some good memories of living in a community vastly different from the ones I've known these last forty years, notable for their well-funded schools, farmers markets, and lack of Negroes. Brenda, like our sons, was raised in such a community. I'm the only member of our family who spent significant years immersed in Black culture, the better aspects of which often compel my reenactment. But my reenactments are nothing, I admit, compared to how one white woman adopted the culture as her own, even going the extra mile of wearing blackface.

Not a literal black face, I should stress, like the kind worn by Ted Danson, Howard Stern, Sarah Silverman, and, to widespread consternation, as he couldn't at least claim poor professional judgment, the prime minister of Canada. But when Justin Trudeau's blackface photos emerged in 2019, he had already established a reputation as an open-minded progressive, so many people were willing to give him a pass, even after his explanation. "The fact is," he said, "I didn't understand how hurtful this is to people who live with discrimination every single day." That was as obvious an untruth as the expectation he would tell one, since feigning ignorance of racist behavior is directly out of the white privilege playbook. The more likely scenario was that as he dug his fingers into a fresh tin of shoe polish, he vacillated between two conflicting thoughts—*This is so awesome* and *This is so wrong*—although those thoughts, it could be argued, were actually in accord, as one of the photos shows him flanked by three fawning women and, three decades later, he was the subject of ridicule and scorn. In any event, he weathered the storm, which was not unexpected because powerful white men seeking, and receiving, second chances is a privilege too.

Rachel Dolezal has not fared as well. She might have at least avoided subsisting primarily on welfare, and her lucrative job offers could have extended beyond reality TV and porn, had her form of blackface been confined to a few hours, rather than fifteen years and counting. She had already been at it for eight in 2015 when a reporter, with a camera recording nearby, thrust a microphone before her and asked if she was African American. The question appeared to stun her, and maybe, if Justin Trudeau had had two thoughts while blacking up, Dolezal, upon her blacking up being exposed, had had but one: *my life is ruined.* It was a life that included being president of the Spokane, Washington, chapter of the NAACP, an instructor of Africana studies at Eastern Washington University, and a police ombudsman, in addition to being a highly regarded and effective civil rights advocate.

Soon all that would be behind her, as behind her, figuratively speaking, as the reporter who watched her stammer and then flee without answering his question.

The answer was this: her parents were white and, when asked about their daughter's race, confirmed she was too. They were ashamed of and embarrassed by her, starting back when as an undergraduate she wore dashikis and head wraps and permed and dyed her hair so that it resembled a curly brown Afro when she was not wearing it in braids. She dated Black men, became impregnated by and married one, attended an HBCU for graduate studies, and, in 2008, bridged the gap between her affinity for blackness and her biological whiteness with makeup. Her skin darkened just enough to be ethnically ambiguous, most people, as is often the default in such circumstances, assumed her to be of African descent.

At first, when new friends and acquaintances sought to confirm this assumption, she gave rambling, convoluted responses about strongly identifying with Black culture and being enlisted in the struggle, but in time that approach gave way to a deception just short of lying, whereby she stated her mother was white. Sometimes the white parent was her father. Eventually the inquiries ceased, which ultimately may have led to her undoing because she lowered her guard and, in the fateful moment with the reporter, faltered. Months later, by the time she had regained her footing enough to describe herself as "transblack," it would be too late for some, and, for others, too absurd.

But for one of her former NAACP colleagues, the description was moot. Her real or perceived race was not the issue, he said, but rather what good she was doing for the Black community. She must have found great comfort in his words, as they were contrary to the ones pummeling her like brass-knuckled fists. "Blackface remains racist," said one critic, "no matter how down with the cause a white person is." Another called her "the undisputed heavyweight champion of cultural appropriation."

That is a title, however, for which there have been many contenders. Elvis comes to mind. So too do Miley Cyrus, Christina Aguilera, Eminem, Justin Timberlake, and Madonna. Madonna, when asked about her cultural appropriations, pulled a page directly from the white privilege playbook too, not by claiming ignorance, like Trudeau, but by claiming privilege itself. "I'm inspired and I'm referencing other cultures," she said. "That is my right as an artist." Change "artist" to "American" and she is also referencing Ralph Ellison.

Ellison wrote in his 1978 essay published in *The American Scholar*, "The Little Man at Chehaw Station":

> *It is here . . . on the level of culture, that the diverse elements of our various backgrounds, our heteroge-neous pasts, have indeed come together, "melted," and undergone metamorphosis. It is here, if we would but recognize it, that elements of the many available tastes, traditions, ways of life, and values that make up the total culture have been ceaselessly appropriated and made their own—consciously, unselfconsciously, or imperialistically—by groups and individuals to*

*whose own backgrounds and traditions they are his-*
*torically alien. Indeed, it was through this process of*
*cultural appropriation (and misappropriation) that*
*Englishmen, Europeans, Africans, and Asians* became
*Americans.*

I suspect Ellison would have defended Madonna, much
as he defended William Styron, whose novel, *The Confes-*
*sions of Nat Turner*, a first-person account of a Black historical figure's failed plot to overthrow slavery, resulted in
Styron vying to be the undisputed heavyweight champion of
cultural appropriation long before Dolezal tossed her hat
into the ring. "William Styron might fail, might have failed,"
Ellison said, "but he has every bit as much right to project
himself into the character of Nat Turner as I have the right to
project myself into the dilemmas of Abraham Lincoln." And
then, projecting himself not into the dilemmas of Abraham
Lincoln, but seemingly into the controversy Dolezal would
spawn fifty years later, Ellison added, "This is not a racial
matter; it is a matter of sensibility, of talent, and of a willingness to become the other." Having but the willingness,
Dolezal, like Styron, resorted to stereotypes.

Dolezal's stereotype is of angry victim of unrelieved racial
oppression. The narrative around her swirled with talk of
hate mail, death threats, nooses hanging outside her house,
and bananas on the hood of her car. "Most of the times she
would speak publicly," said an NAACP member, "she would
speak only of hardship. . . . Every single time she talks about
anything that has to do with her blackness, it's always about

her struggles. And that seemed to be her way of reminding people she's Black." A Black *mother*, to be precise, at the time of two Black sons, whom she once used to dramatize that burden by having them lie on the street, motionless, outlined in chalk, a cringeworthy scene included in the 2018 Netflix documentary of her life, *The Rachel Divide*. With willingness *and* talent and sensibility to become the other, her expression of blackness and Black motherhood would have taken a different form. At minimum, it would have shown the kind of improvisational adaptability to hardship that, in large measure, makes blackness a thing.

Consider, for instance, a 2017 CNN interview with Dolezal. In response to a question about her encounter with the reporter who outed her whiteness, she mused, "If I would have had time to really, you know, discuss my identity, I probably would have described a more complex label: pan-African, pro-Black, bisexual, mother, artist, activist, but I think the question, 'Are you African American?'—I haven't identified as African American. I've identified as Black. And Black is a culture, a philosophy, a political and social view." That would have been the perfect time, it seems to me, for her to crack a sly smile or even laugh out loud at the tragic-comic predicament in which she found herself before producing a cloth and wiping her face clean, thereby perfectly dramatizing her description of blackness, whether or not she truly believed it.

There was a time, I think, that she did. It was when she was a teenager attempting to build the self-esteem of her four recently adopted Black siblings by immersing them in Black history. "A funny thing happened," she said of that process. "I began to feel even more connected to it myself." Connected enough that in college she joined the Black Student Association. She even asked to be one of its officers, which was met with skepticism by many of the club's members. "I delivered an overly earnest speech explaining how passionate I was about Black culture," she later explained, "how I'd always felt a connection with blackness, and about how deeply I cared about my siblings' future." The speech worked. She was approved for the position she sought, which represented her informal induction into the Black community, and from which, fifteen years later, her metamorphosis having given way to minstrelsy, she would be informally expelled.

She described her expulsion as "very painful." Knowing something of what it means to be a part of and apart from the Black community, I believe her to be sincere. "Very painful," however, is not how I describe my circumstance, since I have not been expelled from anything. No one disputes my racial identity. By virtue of my complexion, to say nothing of my birth certificate, my indulgence in Black culture is approved. What I occasionally feel, then, from my outpost of white suburbia, is the intense ache of nostalgia. And when it seizes me, I sometimes soothe it, as I am soothing it now, by watching *Soul Train* videos and throwing down.

But now my imaginary honeys are gone, replaced by a single real one. She is laughing and shaking her head. "You look pretty goofy," Brenda tells me, in response to which I have two conflicting thoughts: *My moves are so awesome* and *My moves are so wrong.*

## MINSTREL II

We were prepared to stop watching Dave Chappelle's comedy special *The Closer* at the first signs of transphobia, but we stopped before reaching any because he kept saying "nigger." Brenda is deeply offended by the word in all instances, whereas I do not mind its casual use, having come of age in a community that allowed for this exception. I also came of age listening to old stand-ups of Richard Pryor, the greatest comedian and n-word-sayer there ever was, although, notably, he did not say it for the last twenty-six years of his life. He renounced it in 1979.

Nineteen seventy-nine was when an overload of stress forced him to take a break from performing. He went to Africa for an extended hiatus, and it was while there, in Nairobi, Kenya, to be exact, as he sat in a hotel lobby, that he had an epiphany he referred to as "magic." A voice popped into his head, he later explained, and commanded him to "look around and tell me what you see." He looked around and told the voice he saw "all shades of brown people doing all kinds of things." "Do you see any niggers?" the voice asked. "No," Pryor responded. "That's because," the voice said, "there aren't any."

Pryor recounted this experience during his 1982 stand-up film *Live on the Sunset Strip*. The audience laughed at first, but it soon realized that this was no laughing matter and fell silent. "And it hit me like a shot," Pryor continued. "I started crying and shit. I was sitting there and I thought I have been here three weeks and I haven't even said it. I haven't even thought it. And it made me say, 'Oh my god, I've been wrong. I've been wrong.'" What he had been wrong about, he felt, was exploiting the word for its easy comedic value, including in the titles of his third and fourth stand-up albums, *That Nigger's Crazy* and *Bicentennial Nigger*, released respectively in 1974 and 1976.

But in 1979, as he sat in that Nairobi hotel lobby, surrounded by people who looked like him, in a country run top to bottom by people who looked like him, he thought, "I've got to regroup my shit. I ain't never going to call another Black man a nigger. You know, because we never was no niggers. That's a word that's used to describe our own wretchedness. And we perpetuate it now." Here the audience clapped and cheered before growing silent once more, for Pryor had begun expressing deep pride in Africa as the cradle of life, the birthplace of humankind. "The first people on Earth were Black," he said. "We the first people who had thought. We the first ones to say, 'Where the fuck am I, and how do you get to Detroit?'" With that, Pryor showed how a comedian could course-correct with grace and humility.

And yet not everyone appreciated him for it. In his 1995 memoir, *Pryor Convictions*, he described how many of his staunchest fans accused him of selling out. Some sent him angry letters; others tossed garbage over the fence surrounding his property. A few even mailed him death threats. His detractors, in other words, saw his course correction as political correctness to the extreme. But Pryor did not care about his detractors. He cared about fulfilling what he saw as his social responsibility. "I no longer wanted to be someone," he wrote, "who pointed out the differences, especially racial ones. I wanted to help people see how similar all of us are. We're all just people, we're all the same."

Members of the LGBTQ+ community offended by *The Closer* believe Dave Chappelle could use a similar course correction. He is certainly capable of it, since he had one before. In 2005, he walked away from his smash-hit comedy series *Chappelle's Show* and a fifty-million-dollar payday because he, like Pryor, concluded that an aspect of his routine was harmful to the Black community. Also like Pryor, Chappelle, overloaded by stress, took a break from performing comedy and went to Africa. Unlike Pryor, however, there was no magic voice awaiting him. His magic voice had facilitated his departure.

It had spoken to him during one of the skits that made him a household name, excluding, somehow, my household. It still puzzles me that I did not become aware of Chappelle until a decade after he quit his show, when I happened upon a skit of his on YouTube. In the skit, he is playing the musician Prince shooting hoops, his game as smooth and dazzling as his guitar riffs despite the fact that he's wearing high heels, dress slacks, and a man-blouse. It was comic genius, I thought, and Prince, reportedly, thought so too. When I managed to stop laughing, I pulled up another of Chappelle's skits, and then another. During the fourth one, Brenda wandered into the room and froze after glancing at my computer the very moment Chappelle appeared in blackface. She abruptly left, on account of being deeply offended, in all instances, by blackface too.

I had not been raised in a community that allowed exceptions for blackface, its casual use or otherwise, and yet I still thought the skit was hysterical. I am chuckling now just recalling it, the gist of which is this: Chappelle's thoughts are manifested as a pixie on his shoulder. The pixie is played by Chappelle as a blackface minstrel, and Chappelle plays himself as an airline passenger. The pixie's appearance on Chappelle's shoulder was prompted by the crisis created when the flight attendant gave Chappelle an entrée choice of fish or chicken. He wants the chicken but, as the only Black person on the plane, and being aware of the stereotype that Blacks are fiendish chicken eaters, he chooses the fish. Then the pixie has its say. *"Wooooweee!"* it bellows. *"I just heard the magic word! Get the chicken! Go on and eat a big bucket, nigger. Take a bite, Black motherfucker!"*

The thought of conforming to racial stereotypes is for many Black people a cause for the kind of crisis experienced by Chappelle's character. It is reasonable, then, that during the rehearsal of the skit, the loudest laughter in the studio would have come from a Black person for whom the crisis was personally familiar, and that this Black person's laughter would have been in sync with the skit's intended funny parts. Instead, the loudest laughter came from a white person, and it came at parts that should not have evoked it. This troubled Chappelle. As he told Oprah in a 2006 interview regarding the incident, "I know the difference between being laughed at and laughed with." He also knew, upon reflection, which is to say upon listening to his magic voice, that he had been "doing sketches that were funny but not socially responsible. I don't want Black people to be disappointed in me for putting that out there." Soon afterward, with grace and humility, a la Richard Pryor, he made the decision to course-correct and embarked to the motherland. *"Wooooweee! Look out, African motherfuckers, cuz here I's come!"*

Chappelle, for the record, said no such thing. I'm just calling him a minstrel as a joke. But the people who called *The Closer* a kind of mean-spirited burlesque were quite serious. For instance, one prominent writer and critic, Roxanne Gay, described the comedy special as "a joyless tirade of incoherent and seething rage, misogyny, homophobia, and transphobia," while another, Saeed Jones, dismissed it as "ashy ideas about gender, queerness, and identity" that are both "harrowing" and "hurtful." By the time I heard these and other condemnations, I had become such a staunch Chappelle fan that I hoped his assessment of his detractors as overly sensitive was true. But I doubted that was the case.

Now, two years later, I am certain it wasn't. This past weekend, Chappelle released another comedy special, *The Dreamer*, and early responses strike a familiar tune. *Rolling Stone* said Chappelle "is apparently incapable of having most of his bits extend beyond mocking genitalia or pronouns. It's not just tired but uninspired." In a review entitled "Dave Chappelle's New Netflix Special Proves He's Learned Nothing," the *Daily Beast* took him to task for devoting so much of his "time and energy to bullying the LGBTQ+ community." Similarly, the *Telegraph* pilloried him for recycling the "same old" anti-trans material "to tiresome effect." At issue, the reviewer contended, was that "the audience is only laughing at the idea that someone else is going to be offended by the material, rather than because it is funny, which, sadly, it isn't."

Sadly, having just watched it, I must agree. Brenda's offense from the n-word still intact, she refused to join me this time, and this time I refused to bail before the end, despite ample reason to do so. I kept expecting the jokes would move beyond the cheap, playground variety to ones sophisticated enough to offer some universal truths about humanity, as he had so often done while portraying Blacks in his comedy skits. It was an expectation raised soon after the release of *The Closer* and the uproar it spawned, when Chappelle, hinting at a course correction, offered to meet with members of the LGBTQ+ community.

There had been no report of this meeting, and it was evident now that it hadn't taken place. But I was certain it would when he made the offer. I had even told Brenda how much I would like to attend it, not only as an ally, but also, selfishly, to try out my joke on Chappelle about him being a minstrel. I thought he would appreciate it, assuming he had not already heard it or something similar. Which he probably had. I know Richard Pryor got wind of the jokes his fans made about him after he accidentally set himself on fire while smoking crack, incurring severe, life-threatening burns. The accident happened in 1980, and two years later, while on stage concluding the taping of *Live on the Sunset Strip*, he told the audience, "Y'all did some nasty-ass jokes on my ass." Then he demonstrated one by striking a match and bouncing it through the air. "What's that?" he asked. "Richard Pryor running down the street." Laughter filled the auditorium. Pryor sneered, turned to exit the stage, and then, because he truly did know the difference between being laughed with and being laughed at, he paused to crack a smile.

## A DOCTOR NEAR ME

For two years after my doctor retired, I forestalled the drudgery of finding a new one, which was good for my hypochondria but not my marriage. When the day finally arrived that Brenda refused to hear another word about my growing list of symptoms, even though some *could* lead to very bad outcomes, I forced myself to google "doctors near me" and called the first name on the list. So here I am, a month later, pulling in the parking lot of the Mackall Group, which, according to the building's marquee, consists of a single Mackall named George.

The building itself is two stories and appears to be in the final stages of construction. Painters and landscapers touch up the exterior; half the parking lot remains to be paved. A handwritten note taped to the door directs visitors past the unoccupied first floor and up a flight of stairs that opens into a lobby. Two people are waiting. A receptionist sitting behind a counter looks up from her desk as I reach her. I tell her my name. After typing it into her computer, she cheerfully says, "I see it's your first time with us. Oh, you'll *love* Dr. Mackall!"

"And Dr. Mackall," I say, to match the unlikeliness of her

claim, "will love *me*." Aside from the hypochondria, I can be a difficult patient, which is to say I question everything my health-care provider does, including, for instance, describing himself in the plural form. I inquire about the marquee.

"Yes, Dr. Mackall is the only member of the group so far," she responds. "He just started his private practice, but once it expands, the signage will already be in place without him spending another penny."

He is forward-thinking; I like that. And optimistic. But his frugality is concerning. While he surely spent a fortune to build his facility in this wealthy town, did he hire top-of-the-line staff? Does he have a competent answering service? Is his equipment state-of-the-art? I scan the room, attempting to ascertain the quality of the décor and the patients. Both, from what I can tell, look high-end, especially the sleek leather chairs, two art deco lamps, the young man in the tweed business suit, and the middle-aged woman nestling a Chanel purse with bejeweled fingers. Of the magazines splayed on a table, I can make out the cover of one from my distance: the *New Yorker*. I breathe a little easier. And yet, there is room in a far corner, I cannot help but notice, for a cappuccino maker and a mini fridge stocked with bottles of Voss and Perrier, as was the case in my previous doctor's lobby. Maybe Dr. Mackall is holding off for the rest of the group before going all in.

The receptionist hands me a questionnaire attached to a clipboard. Just as I settle into a chair, the door leading from the office's interior opens and a woman emerges who looks to be in her seventies, followed by a man of similar age. Like the two people waiting and the receptionists, the woman is white, which I note only because the man is Black, which I note only because he is wearing a lab coat, which means that George, my potential new doctor, is a brother. "You have a nice day now," he says to the woman, who bids him the same. And then, before retreating out of view, he and I briefly make eye contact, during which I may or may not mouth, "I love you."

Yes, I love him, I do not mind saying, because he is Black. And what I love about his blackness is that I did not seek him out for it; our encounter is based solely on his office's proximity to my house and his credentials. I, too, love his credentials. I have found few things more pride-inducing than chancing upon Black people in elite professions. The first (and still only) time I boarded a plane and saw a Black woman in the cockpit, I nearly fist-pumped; likewise, when I learned that a Black man with whom I struck up a conversation in a Starbucks was an architect. My heart even swelled a little that one time when, in my misspent youth, I had the occasion to visit a criminal defense law firm and saw, on the portrait wall of distinguished past partners, a bespectacled Black man who, fortunately, was not there in the flesh to see me discrediting the race. I would like to think I am a credit to it now, and I suspect, on the rare instance some of my colleges' few Black students chance upon me as their professor, their hearts swell a little with pride too.

I turn my attention back to the questionnaire, though only briefly, for I cannot help but wonder about the two other people waiting. Were they aware of Dr. Mackall's race before they met him? Had they sought him out because of it? Not unthinkable, I know, but also not likely. What is likely is that upon discovering his race they would have found it necessary to seek care elsewhere. I have heard of this happening. I have also heard of emergency room patients refusing to be seen by the Black physician who arrives to treat if not to save them. And yet, here are this man and woman, willingly placing themselves in the care of Brother Mackall, and this, in some small way, makes me proud of them too.

The interior door opens again, and a nurse peers from behind it to call a name. The man rises and follows her. A few moments after I return to my questionnaire, the nurse is back for the woman. That's an impressive turnaround, I think, before picking up the pace of my responses. I fly through the rest of the questionnaire and return it to the receptionist. Ten minutes later, the nurse comes for me. I follow her down a winding corridor and into an examination room. She is not much of a talker, which is fine, except that I must ask for the results of my vitals rather than simply be told them. Surprisingly, they are in the normal range of a healthy adult, thereby eliminating a half-dozen possible afflictions on my list. She hands me a gown. "Underwear and socks stay on," she says before leaving.

Once gowned, I sit on the examination table for fifteen minutes, staring at the blank walls. Next, for variety's sake, I stare at the ceiling. After another five minutes pass, I get my phone and catch up on emails. When that's done, I check the time; I've been in here for twenty-five minutes. I open my Twitter app to read Trump's latest racist comments, which takes twenty minutes more and feeds into the anger the wait has begun to produce. I text Brenda so she can calm me down. "Forty-five minutes in the examination room," I write. "No doctor yet."

"That's outrageous," she responds, which is as calming as that new mole on my arm.

"Really?" I write.

"Really."

"Maybe he's dealing with an emergency?"

"Someone would have told you."

"Overbooked?"

"No excuse."

"What should I do?"

"Find a nurse."

"Can't."

"Why not?"

"I'm naked."

"Should you be?"

There is a rattle outside my door: my chart being removed from the bin. I type "He's here" and toss my phone on top of my clothes, piled next to me on one of two chairs. Another rattle, followed by silence. Was my chart . . . *returned*? I let a few moments pass before getting my phone. I type, "I lied."

"About your nakedness I hope."

Smiling, I type. "Maybe." And maybe, I think, as my smile fades, Dr. Mackall's blackness is a lie too. He could be an Oreo, one of those Negroes who, by virtue of their elite profession, feels removed from the race. I have also seen this before, and if I am seeing it now, the last thing he wants, I know, is a Black patient. That would explain why he opened his practice in a white community. It would also explain, it suddenly dawns on me, that he's making me wait this long in hopes that I will leave. Or, worse, if he thinks that I *did* seek him out because he is Black, he is certain I *won't* leave, thereby freeing him up to dote on his white patients. . . .

There is another rattle, though fainter this time: the examination room, I deduce, next door. Voices, briefly, in the hall. I get my phone again. "I caught a glimpse of the doctor earlier," I type to Brenda. "He's Black."

"And?"

"On the outside."

"What?"

"He's an Oreo. Possibly double-stuffed."

"Don't find a nurse."

"Why not?"

"Find a psychiatrist."

"I'm serious!"

She does not respond, which is her response. I turn off my phone. I'll get dressed and leave, I decide, if he's not here in five minutes, give or take ten. The woman with the purse *did* look a little sickly, now that I think about it; perhaps he's consoling her after breaking some devastating news. If true, or if there is some other legitimate reason why he is so delayed, my seeking out a nurse would put me in a bad light. An even worse light would be if I appear to expect preferential treatment, as if I, Brother Walker, do not believe I should have to wait like his white patients. Assuming, that is, as I am not prepared to do, that his white patients have to wait.

I check the time: two minutes past my five-minute deadline plus the ten-minute cushion. I have been in this examination room for an hour and a half. I put on my clothes.

The hall is empty, but I can hear voices around the corner near the door leading to the lobby. I recognize one of the voices as Dr. Mackall's just before he comes into view. He is standing next to the sickly woman, their backs to me as they face the receptionist, who sees me and immediately understands. "Mr. Walker!" she says, rising. "Dr. Mackall was *just* headed in to see you."

Dr. Mackall whirls around, already looking embarrassed. He holds up a finger to say "One second" and then turns back to the woman. "Your prescription has been sent," he tells her. "I'll see you back here in six months?"

"Yes, doctor, six months. Thank you."

They shake hands before Dr. Mackall faces me again. "I'm so sorry for the delay," he says, taking a step toward my examination room. "Please, come, come." Behind him, the woman opens the door and leaves. It would not be unreasonable for me to leave as well, but that would escalate Dr. Mackall's embarrassment to humiliation, which, I'm surprised to discover, I'm not prepared to do either. I follow him to the examination room.

As we sit across from each other in the two chairs, I expect him to apologize again and offer some implausible explanation for his delay, but this would be inconsistent with his smile, which is so genuine-looking that it makes me think that I am upset for no reason, that an hour-and-a-half wait is normal. "It's really nothing to be concerned about," I imagine him saying. "It's common, and completely harmless."

"So, Mr. Walker," he says instead, "tell me about yourself. What do you do for a living?"

"I'm a professor," I say, even though that's listed on the chart he's holding.

"Is that right? What do you teach?"

"Literature and creative writing."

"I'll have to watch my grammar!" he responds with a laugh. "You know," he continues, now settling back into his chair, "I had this English teacher once, this was in high school, many, many years ago, long before you were born, and she used to make us write these essays based on five random words. Five random words! See, all the students would write a word on a slip of paper, and she'd pass around a paper bag and have us put our word in it, and after giving the bag a good shake, she'd pull out five words and write them on the board. Then we had to write a coherent paragraph that incorporated those words! I remember this one time that a kid next to me wrote . . ."

I half-listen to what the kid next to him wrote. And then I half-listen to how the kid later died in an apartment fire, and how that kid and the apartment fire remind him of the fires currently raging in California, which had always been on his wish list of places to live, but who in their right mind would want to live there now, between the fires and the rising temperatures, but he'll never move back to Kansas, where he was born and raised, on account of the growing frequency of tornados, which is a segue for his thoughts I half-listen to on global warming, though he is not sure, he says, with apologies to my political leanings if I find this offensive, that the

Green New Deal is the solution, but he nonetheless admires many aspects of it, and as I half-listen to these admirable aspects, I understand that what I worried about him is wrong. I have not had to wait because he is a double-stuffed Oreo. I have had to wait because he is a chatterbox. I am not sure which is worse.

But I am sure I will not return. Since I'm already here, however, I will go through with my physical. That will give me another year, maybe two, depending on the extent of Brenda's patience, and provided none of my remaining symptoms pan out, before I must embark on this drudgery again.

## IT'S HARD OUT HERE
## FOR A MEMOIRIST

For longtime memoirists, there invariably comes a point when the material runs a little thin, forcing them to make use of their most guarded secrets and transgressions, as I shall do here. To begin, then, once, many years ago, when I was seventeen, and for a very brief period, merely seven weeks, to be exact, I was a pimp. I am deeply ashamed of this. It helps to remind myself that what primarily appealed to me about the profession were the fedoras and flashy cars, as well as the possibility of having many girlfriends, or at least one. And I especially liked the idea of not working, or rather, as my older brother Tim used to say, not working for "the man." Tim had worked for the man once and strongly advised against it. There were much better options, he said, but the ones he recommended, alas, were not those.

He would admit to having steered me wrong, I believe, if he could. Tragically, he succumbed to some of the very vices he taught me, his heart, overtaxed by the strains of street life and probably regret, giving out at age forty-seven. The manner of his premature death could not have been predicted by anyone who knew him in his youth: honors student, religious to the point of fanaticism, loving, witty, and kind. And then, overnight, it seemed, he was running hustles and cons before dropping out of college and quitting his part-time job as an accountant. But I do wonder sometimes if it was not regret that played a role in his death. Maybe it was the blame he harbored for whomever had led him astray. The idea to live outside the law, after all, could not have come to him on its own, any more than it had come to me.

How it had come to me was this: I was engrossed in one of my sister's romance novels, fretting over the heroine's decision to elope with her fiancée's father, when Tim, nineteen, snatched the book from my hands. He had done this before. Romance novels, he suspected, were improper reading material for fourteen-year-old Black boys, and my friends had proved his suspicion to be true. They had recently discovered one on my dresser, my sister's feathered bookmark fanning from its pages, and the ensuing teasing was merciless. I never brought the novels to my bedroom again. Instead, I hid them in the garage where, every day after school, I would unearth one and sit on a blanket behind our parents' defunct station wagon to enter into faraway worlds of love and desire, always alert to the sound of approaching footsteps, which, on the day in question, escaped me. "Here," Tim said, dropping a book onto my lap. "Read *this*." I looked at the title. It was *Pimp: The Story of My Life*, by Iceberg Slim. I returned it to him a few days later.

"What did you think?" he asked.

"I think," I said, "I should not have read that."

He disagreed. There was another author, he added, with whom I should also be familiar. His name was Donald Goines. Goines had been a pimp too. He had also been a bootlegger, thief, addict, and inmate, so he had plenty of material at his disposal, enough to fill sixteen novels. I should not have read those either. And he probably should not have written them. It was believed that a number of the people on whom he had based his characters objected to their portrayal and rendered the harshest of critiques. Goines's body, along with his girl-friend's, was found in his apartment, full of bullets.

Some memoirists, in an effort to juice up the narrative tension, would exaggerate the gulf between their experiences and those of Donald Goines and Iceberg Slim, but the fact of the matter is if my avatar were an animal, it would have been, for the first eleven years of my life, Bambi. I knew nothing beyond church, Marvel Comics, the Three Stooges, and, when I turned twelve, but only in strict obedience to the de-mands of nature, the lingerie section of the Sears catalog. Did I press my mouth upon the models' tiny faces? Did I rub my fingers along their miniature bosoms? Did I hold those pages up to the light, hoping to discover the mysteries beyond the discounted silks and satins? I did. Quite often. Obsessively, some might say. This, however, was hardly preparation for entering the worlds of Donald Goines and Iceberg Slim, al-though the worlds of Donald Goines and Iceberg Slim, in retrospect, would have been good preparation for entering the backyard of Rachel Jones. Rachel was a new girl on our block. Rumor had it she liked being felt up.

I provided a detailed account of my confirmation of this

rumor in my second memoir; suffice it here for the reader to picture Bambi getting his first whiff of smoke as the forest burns, for I, like that delicate creature, after willing my trembling, fourteen-year-old self beneath the raised deck where the seventeen-year-old had lured me, was suddenly paralyzed with fear and indecision. Rachel relieved me of both by guiding my hands.

And yet that did not prepare me for the worlds of Donald Goines and Iceberg Slim either. Nor did the dirty magazine a classmate had pilfered from his father's stash and brought to school, nor the one I discovered while rummaging through my sister's bedroom, and certainly not her romance novels, although the one about the pilot and three stewardesses was helpful. In combination, however, these items awakened in me a strong curiosity about manhood and how I might enter into it. I read the books Tim gave me, then, partially in search of answers. More often I found questions. I recall after reading only the first paragraph of *Pimp* asking my twin brother, "What's a 'hairy maw'?" He shrugged. I offered to show him the passage for context, but not being much of a reader, he declined. Besides, he was busy completing the homework Tim had assigned us, which was to roll joints with tree leaves. Once we mastered that, Tim had said, we could try it with actual marijuana.

When writing about certain subsets of American culture, one of the memoirist's great challenges is to draw a distinction between bad decisions and bad people. Tim was not a bad person. He had merely taken the pulse of the community we'd recently moved to, foreseen the swift demographic change from white and middle-class to Black and impoverished, and hoped to immunize his younger brothers against the coming surge of crime by injecting small amounts of it into our bloodstream. In a sense, this is similar to the practice I had heard of wealthy people serving their underage children wine with dinner, as if in so doing, the children, having surmised Bordeaux is as innocuous as Ovaltine, would decide against becoming alcoholics. The unlucky among them, of course, are wrong, for something in their constitution awakens a craving for booze, all of which is to say that, after deducing the meaning of "hairy maw," I was curious to learn more.

Fortunately, this was the 1970s and '80s, the golden age of Black street cinema. A few classics still ran in theaters, but bootlegged copies were easy to find. My friends and I started with *The Mack* and *Sweet Sweetback's Baadasssss Song* before moving on to *Shaft*, *Trick Baby*, *Willie Dynamite*, and, of course, *Superfly*. *Superfly* was our favorite. We watched it again and again, our admiration growing each time for the main character, Youngblood Priest, as he snorted cocaine while winding through ghetto streets in his El Dorado, his pressed hair falling like silk from his fedora, his lush mustache curling down his upper lip in perpetual disdain of the shit that he, a Black man, had to overcome. Priest was a god to us all.

Others thought he was the devil. NAACP leader Junius Griffin, for instance, the man who coined the term "blaxploitation," railed against the genre on the grounds that it perpetuated stereotypes of Blacks as criminals. Black men in particular, in the words of another objector, were celebrated for having "vast physical prowess but no cognitive skills." Protestors picketed theaters holding signs that read "Black Shame, White Profits" and "We Are Not All Pimps and Whores!" Cars in movie theater parking lots were fire-bombed. But there were advocates of the genre, too, who applauded African Americans' increased participation in the film industry and referred to the movies as mere action flicks. Gordon Parks Sr., director of *Shaft*, thought audiences should be given enough credit to know the difference between fantasy and reality. It was his son, however, Gordon Parks Jr., who offered the genre's best defense: "Blacks want to be entertained just like everyone else," he argued, "and if they enjoy superheroes with fast cars and fancy clothes, well, that's the American dream—*everyone's* American dream."

*Right on.* Because at that time on the South Side of Chicago, these superheroes felt vital for the heroic twist they put on the Black man's bleak plight. And what they perpetuated was our understanding that this plight could be transcended, which was to say it was possible to avoid selling out and working for the man. All we had to be was cunning. We had to be bold. We had to be ruthless. Above all, we had to look good.

I pressed my hair and bought a fedora. I perfected my stride and learned to talk with a toothpick balanced on my lower lip. I memorized the scripts of a dozen cons and hustles. When my Superfly avatar was fully formed, I hit the streets ready to lay claim to their riches, but the streets, I soon discovered, had scripts of their own. The one they wrote for me was a fawn who masquerades as a buck and gets in so far over his head that he ruins a decade of his life, and for this, years later, once I became a memoirist, I was grateful. So bountiful were my failings and misdeeds that when I wrote my first memoir, I could pick and choose what to include without fear of depleting my material. I withheld enough to spruce up much of my second memoir and a collection of personal essays. And never once, in any of these accounts, for reasons of propriety and discretion, which were still good options for me then, did I mention Thelma Ellsworth.

I am tempted, in the common manner of memoirists, to cast myself in an exceedingly favorable light by describing Thelma as breathtakingly beautiful, like Pam Grier in *Foxy Brown*, or Tamara Hall in *Cleopatra Jones*, or Marki Bey in *Sugar Hill*, but it is important to note that no such woman would have had me. I leave it to the reader to imagine the woman who, at age thirty-one, would have had a seventeen-year-old high school dropout whose money, on the rare occasion he had it, was ill-gotten, who was a heavy user of drugs and alcohol, and who, incidentally, was high on both when he fell down a flight of stairs and ended up in an emergency room, thereby facilitating this chance encounter. Thelma was a nurse's aide. "I like your style," she said while bandaging my wrist.

I acknowledged the compliment with a slight adjustment to my fedora.

"What do you do," she asked, "sell dope?"

"Naw, *baby*," I said. "I'm a *pimp*!"

"Is that so?"

"Damn *right!*"

"Pimp," she said, smiling, "was my second guess."

"Really?"

"The toothpick gave you away. And your *smoothness.*"

I adjusted my fedora again. A short while later, after I had, as we used to say, "spit my game," by which I mean repeated pickup lines I'd heard in various blaxploitation films, she gave me her number.

I had been chosen.

"Chosen?" Tim said, when I told him. "By who, and for what?"

"By this woman," I said, "to be her *pimp.*"

"*Boy*, are you high?"

"Yes."

"Me too," he said. "Tell me more."

I did, but first I reminded him of the scene in *The Mack* where the protagonist, Goldie, who had just been released from prison after a five-year stint, was at a bar when a female friend joined him for a drink. As they chatted, she revealed she had been working as a prostitute. The job was not optimal, she admitted, but the main drag was the harassment she received from pimps for being an independent contractor. "You know," she explained, "I'm an outlaw, and a lot of pimps are down on me because I won't choose. But Goldie, you know, I *need* a man. I need *somebody* in my corner. Somebody to *be* there. Help me, Goldie. I'm tired of being by myself."

"Thelma," I continued, "this woman I met, is tired of being by herself. She needs *somebody in her corner.*"

"She said that?" Tim asked.

"More or less, after I told her I was a pimp."

"You *told her* you were a pimp?"

"It seemed the thing to do at the time."

"Then what?"

"I spit my game."

"And then?"

"She gave me her number."

"She chose you, alright," Tim responded. "You know what to do now, don't you?"

"No," I said. "That's why I'm calling."

"Boy, didn't you read Donald Goines and Iceberg Slim?"

"That was a long time ago. And, to be honest, they were kind of confusing. Also, Thelma's not a *prostitute* prostitute, you know, other than working for the man."

"It's all the same. As long as she's making you that money!"

"Hell, yeah!"

"The main thing," he recommended, "is to play it cool."

"I did," I said. "I told her I'd have to *think* about calling her, just like Goldie told his lady friend."

"Good, good. The longer you play it cool, the better."

I played it cool for three days. When I called her, she invited me to her apartment for dinner. Two days later, I returned home to get my things.

Pimping was easy. All I did after driving Thelma to work was to pick up a few of my friends in her ten-year-old Pinto and head to the park to shoot hoops or get high. Sometimes we would simply grab a pint of wine and go to her apartment to play Pong. Her shift ended at 11:00 PM, so a little before then I would drive to the hospital to get her. She would be waiting for me outside the entrance with some of her female coworkers. They smiled and giggled as she got into the car.

A month into the life, she took me shopping for new clothes. Her fondness for floral shirts and tight slacks was not one I shared, but we were on the same page when it came to fedoras. She bought me seven, each a different color, one for every day of the week. Sometimes, because she had a good eye for these things, she would match one of the fedoras with one of the shirts she selected for me to wear. My friends were impressed with my new look. Tim, however, was skeptical. But what got his approval was when I told him that Thelma finally agreed to call me "Daddy." "Daddy," she had said, "don't forget to pick up my dry cleaning."

"I won't," I'd responded.

"You forgot last week. And the week before that."

I took out my toothpick and said, "Don't hassle me, woman, about my *memory*."

"You got the grocery list?" she asked.

I was driving her to work. "Yes."

"Oh, we getting low on milk too. I forgot to add that."

"Okay."

"*Whole* milk, now. You know I don't like that two-percent shit you bought last time."

"I know, I know. Whole milk."

"And check the date."

"*Damn*, woman. You finished getting on *my case*?"

She smiled and asked, "You need any money, *Daddy*?"

It was only Wednesday, but I had just seven dollars left

from the thirty she gave me each Monday. "I could use a little more," I said. She gave me a little more.

After dropping her off, I drove to Tim's apartment. He wasn't there, so I tracked down two of my friends. We smoked a joint before heading to the liquor store to get a couple of forties. The liquor store was near the taverns where some big-time pimps hung out. Their cars lined the street, Lincolns and Cadillacs, but not the Rolls Royce that belonged to the legendary Magellan because, according to the grapevine, he was in intensive care after being stabbed by one of his women. Since it was unlikely that I would be stabbed by Thelma, I preferred my brand of pimping to his. It would have been nice, though, to have one of those sweet rides.

I would get one in a few months, after I moved back home and started working for the man. Tim would say that I had sold out, which, strictly speaking, would be true, but it would not be like I'd had better choices. Thelma would throw me out after the last time I forgot her dry cleaning and fucked up the grocery shopping, as I was about to do that night. I remembered the dry cleaning at around 9:00, two hours after the cleaners had closed, but I still had time to make it to the grocery store. I hurried there after dropping off my friends. In the parking lot, before getting out of the car, I checked myself in the rearview mirror. I smiled. I looked good.

The store was busy, unusual for a Wednesday night. Maybe there was some kind of a sale, I thought, but I had not seen notice of one earlier while clipping the coupons that, I just realized, were still on the kitchen table. The grocery list was there too. Now I would have to try to jog my memory by going down every aisle. That was how I ended up in the one with the magazines, which was also the one with the paperbacks, which happened to include the romance novels I used to borrow from my sister. They stopped me in my tracks.

Did I put six in the cart? Did I hide them beneath the dresser to read while Thelma was at work? Did I, overcome by nostalgia, and in sad recognition of an innocence long lost, bookmark the pages with a feather from one of my fedoras? And did I cry, on occasion, at the terrible direction my life had taken and blame my poor, misguided brother? No. I did none of these things. But the urge was there. I would have acted on it, too, had I known I would become a memoirist. I could have used those scenes.

# MASTER OF THE LAWN

This story is different from other stories. You and YOU ALONE are in charge of what happens. YOU must beware of racists, paranoia, self-pity, anger, and white privilege while using all your heroism, survival strategies, and some of your sense of humor. The wrong decision could result in disaster—even death. But don't despair. At any time, YOU can go back and make another choice, alter the direction of your story, and change its result. Here is the scenario: you are a middle-aged Black man living in a wealthy, predominately white town, about to mow your lawn.

Good luck.

## 1

Earlier this summer, for the first time in your life, you hired landscapers. The most recent one lasted three weeks before you fired him, as you fired his two predecessors, for repeatedly mowing your lawn so low as to create divots. And because all of these landscapers were white, you cannot rule out the possibility that their poor service was related to your race.

If it was not race-related, perhaps they were only seeking to amuse themselves and never considered that someone driving past as you are mowing would slow down, survey your apparent incompetence, and then look at you and yell a racial slur. That may have just happened. You would not bet your life on it, however, because the traffic noise obscured most of the man's words, leaving you certain of only his first, which was "Nice."

If you decide the man yelled, "Nice day for doing the lawn, I see!" skip to paragraph 8.

If you decide the man yelled, "Nice way to ruin the lawn, blacky!" go to paragraph 2.

**2**

Another racist! As a matter of pride, you must go after him, but, as a matter of prudence, you must not. Luckily there is a loophole; your car is low on gas and the Shell station is in the direction the man is headed. You can "go after him" and, if he "escapes," fill up.

**3**

You rush to your car and pull to the end of the driveway where, because you live on Main Street, a stream of vehicles brings you to a halt. Main Street, by appearance and official designation, is a highway, not the "convenient thoroughfare" described by the Realtor who sold you the house. On many occasions you have waited at the end of your driveway for a break in the traffic for over a minute. Now, during the first thirty seconds, the vision of you confronting the driver is slowly replaced by the vision of the last driver you confronted. Was he also a racist? Maybe. But he did not make this explicit by calling you a blacky. He called you a sonofabitch.

### 4

That happened a decade ago as you entered the intersection of a four-way stop. The other driver was doing the same from your left, but he should not have been because you arrived seconds before him. Had he thought that because he was white, he had the right of way? Was this just some more white privilege bullshit? You still wonder about this. You also still wonder if you could live with yourself if you ignored white privilege bullshit when it was directly invoked at your expense. Perhaps one day you will know. "Go fuck yourself!" you responded, momentarily forgetting that your ten- and twelve-year-old sons were in the back seat, not good ages to hear you give this advice. You realized that even before your wife glared at you from the passenger seat. You realized, too, that she had given wise counsel when she urged you to simply let the man go, right before the collision.

### 5

You and the man got out of your cars to inspect the damage. Yours was minimal: a small dent in the front bumper. His rear passenger door, however, was cratered where you plowed into it. He was furious. So were you. But you were not high on meth or acid or whatever it was that had him suddenly abandon your shouting match and begin pacing, flailing his arms, and muttering to himself before going all bug-eyed when your wife appeared at your side and told you to call the police. Then he stopped pacing and calmly said, "Hey, listen folks, your car is fine, so why don't we forget it?" Then you snickered and said, "So you admit that *I* had the right of way?" Then your wife poked you in the ribs and said "Get in the car."

## 6

And that was the end of that, on the one hand. On the other hand, you lost a lot of sleep that night thinking about the poor example you set for your sons. On the *other* other hand, you had shown them how to deal with racists, which, to be fair, the man may not have been. The man you are going after now may not be either. It is possible, after all, that he did say it was a nice day for doing the lawn. Would it absolutely *kill* you to believe this?

If you decide it would absolutely kill you to believe this, jump to paragraph 12.

If you decide it would not absolutely kill you to believe this, continue to paragraph 7.

## 7

You park your car and resume mowing your lawn, delighted at how good you suddenly feel for giving a potential racist the benefit of the doubt. In terms of plot, this is not much of a story; however, as a Black man merely feeling good in a public space, it is all the story you ever need. You are pleased that it ends here.

## 8

It's the *perfect* day, actually, for doing the lawn. Warm, dry, light breeze, and partially sunny, exactly how you like it. If only you had a John Deere E180 26HP riding lawn mower with a V-twin engine and a beer holder. With one of those bad boys, you would be able to make quick work of this chore while staying hydrated and enjoying the weather—*if*, that is, the mower would not topple over due to your lawn's dangerously steep slope and sever one of your legs. Even your puny electric mower sometimes threatens to topple over. This is the only reason you forced yourself to hire landscapers in the first place; a man, in your estimation, should never hire another man to cut his own lawn, unless a leg is at stake.

## 9

You recently touched on this point with one of your neighbors. You like this particular neighbor a great deal because, in addition to being friendly, he, unlike most men you see in this town, cuts his own lawn and shares your low regard of men who do not. He is also the neighbor who told you about the guy who severed his leg on your slope a couple of years before you bought your house. His mower had not toppled over; rather, he had toppled over while carrying a large tree branch and somehow got caught in his chipper. The point, though, is that your slope is dangerous. So you know your neighbor did not hold it against you when he saw your parade of landscapers, but you might hold it against him when you suddenly notice a MAGA sign rising from his petunias.

If you decide to hold your neighbor's MAGA sign against him, go to paragraph 11.

If you decide not to hold your neighbor's MAGA sign against him, go to the next paragraph.

## 10

The MAGA movement, you are well aware, is based on racist and white supremacist ideology. You understand, therefore, that to not hold this against its members would put you in the company of Black people whom many consider to be traitors to the race, like Kanye West, "Blacks for Trump," and Ali Alexander, that peculiar-looking brother who once claimed to be in contact with the Proud Boys and the Oath Keepers.

If you want to join the company of race traitors, you can go fuck yourself, because your story ends here.

If you do not want to join the company of race traitors, go to paragraph 11.

## 11

You are getting pissed. Every time you look at that MAGA sign, you can almost feel your blood pressure rising. After a dozen or so looks, you have become short of breath—an indication that you may be on the verge of a stroke. You know you should take a break in order to vent to your wife because she has a way of talking you down when you get like this. But you are not in the mood to be talked down. You are in the mood to be pissed, even if it kills you. So you keep mowing and looking at the sign, all while ignoring the voice in your head urging you to give your neighbor the benefit of the doubt because maybe he supports Trump solely for his tax breaks and his views on border security. You are also ignoring your neighbor, who has come out onto his porch. He waves at you. You look from him to his sign and then back at him. He waves again. You look at his sign once more before once more looking at him and this time when he waves you wave in return, not to acknowledge your friendship, but, as you'll never speak to him again, to bid it goodbye. Your story ends here.

## 12

You have been searching the neighborhood for ten minutes without success. The racist has escaped. You are not surprised, given the record ninety-three seconds it took you to exit your driveway. In all honesty, you are relieved about the extended delay because it gave you time to try out some of that amateur therapy your wife likes to practice on you. *Why do you think*, you asked yourself, *it is not in your best interest to go after this man?* To that, you responded, *Because he could have a gun.* But your strong comeback to that was *That's why I need one!* After all, you reasoned, with the rise of the MAGA movement, white folks have been acting crazy.

You want to be prepared for when they completely lose their marbles. That is why, if there is anything in the world you want—besides, that is, a John Deere E180 26HP riding lawn mower with a V-twin engine and a beer holder—it is a Beretta M92 semiautomatic pistol.

## 13

As far as you can tell, the one big downside to owning a Beretta M92 semiautomatic pistol, which is also its one big upside, is that you would use it. Imagine if you had had one that night at the high school musical! That was in 2015, when your friends' daughter was cast in a production of *Les Misérables* and invited your family to attend the opening performance. You had gotten a late start; by the time you arrived at the campus, its parking lot was nearly full. The ticket line trailed out the door. Your family had not long reached the line's end before you noticed, through the lobby's window, that your friends were already inside, gesturing at you. They held up a batch of tickets, indicating that they had purchased yours. So your family joined them. Seconds later someone tapped you on the shoulder. You turned to see an old white man, his face beet red. "No *line-jumping*!" he snapped. "Who do you *think* you are?"

## 14

Who you thought you were was one of four Black people—your wife and two sons being the other three—in that massive white crowd, and therefore a prime target for some white privilege bullshit. Who you *knew* you were was a man.

Everyone in the immediate vicinity fell silent, waiting, no doubt, to see if this were true, including your sons. They were only eleven and thirteen, too young to see you shove a senior citizen to the floor, so you told him, if it was *any* of his business, which it was not, that your friends had already purchased your tickets. "I don't give a damn," he responded. "*Get* to end of the line!" That was the exact moment, if you'd owned a Beretta M92 semiautomatic pistol, you would have shot him. Instead, you advised him of what he could go do with himself, and that was the exact moment, your wife later said, he could have shot you. But apparently he did not have a Beretta M92 semiautomatic pistol either. Nor did he have the courage of his conviction. After a brief stare-down, he turned and walked away.

## 15

Your evening was ruined. You almost salvaged it during the students' rendition of "Master of the House," the innkeeper's charming ditty that always made you smile and sing along, but now, when you belted out "Master . . . ," your thoughts returned to the old man, how he must have longed for a time when that word had but one meaningful reference. He was no doubt the kind of guy who had found a prominent place on his lawn to mount a MAGA sign. Every time you see one, you still think of that man. You think of him now while filling up at the Shell station near a car with a MAGA bumper sticker, and you think of him again when you arrive home to discover, after you resume mowing, a MAGA sign rising from your friendly neighbor's petunias. You will not tell your wife about going after that other racist, but you will definitely tell her about discovering this one.

### 16

You storm into the house, already so pissed off it is difficult to speak. When your wife manages to decipher your words, she asks, "Why do you think it's not in your best interest to get worked up about a stupid MAGA sign?" This is a trap you fail to recognize; as soon as you lower your head and mumble, "Because I could have a stroke," she mentions seeing two other MAGA signs around the corner. Unbelievable, you think, as you head back outside to your mower. What's this wealthy white town coming to? Then again, its ratio of "Black Lives Matter" signs to MAGA signs is probably twenty to one. And there had been that golden period two years ago, brought on by the vile murder of George Floyd, where the ratio may have risen as high as forty to one. Those months of public support for the importance of your race were heartwarming, without question, but the thing that genuinely moved you during that period was what you happened upon early one Sunday morning.

### 17

You had been driving in a light rain to the waste station when you noticed, standing along Main Street, a lone white child, no more than seven or eight, holding a large piece of cardboard high over his head. His back was to you, so he did not see you approaching, and you could not yet read his sign. When you passed him and could read his sign—"Black Lives

Matter"—it was too late to respond. You hoped he would still be there ten minutes later when you returned, and he was. Only he was facing your opposite direction again. This time as you approached, you reduced your speed, lowered your window, and then extended a thumbs-up before beeping your horn. The boy spun around and, seeing you, leaped for joy. This memory warms your heart. Your faith in humanity is renewed.

## 18

But maybe not for long. Ten minutes after you resume mowing, a middle-aged white woman pulls her car into your driveway. She waves you over. You turn off your mower and approach her with trepidation. When you are a few feet away, she asks, "What do you charge to cut a lawn this size?"

If you decide to maintain your renewed faith in humanity, skip to paragraph 20.

If you decide not to maintain your renewed faith in humanity, go to paragraph 19.

## 19

"I'm *not* a damn landscaper," you say. Flustered, the woman apologizes while fumbling to put her gear in reverse. As you back away from her idling car (she is blocked in by the traffic), you impulsively begin a review of the many encounters during your lifetime you have had like this, including being mistaken for a valet, a security guard, a doorman, and, despite being only five-nine and of slight build, a Boston Celtic. By the time you finish mowing, you are pretty worked up again. Sadly, for you are an incorrigible hothead, you will continue to get pretty worked up over every stupid racist thing and are all but certain to die young of a stroke. Could that, on some subconscious level, be your intent? It's a deeply troubling hypothesis, and an important one for you to ponder as your story concludes.

## 20

"I charge," you tell the woman, "two hundred dollars." The woman says, "That's kind of high." You disagree, on account of the lawn's dangerously steep slope. She does not have a dangerously steep slope, she responds, so you reduce your fee by thirty dollars. This makes her smile, or maybe she is smiling because you are smiling. You struggle not to do more than smile, but you bust up laughing when she asks about the divots. "Sorry," you tell her, composing yourself, "but it's amusing when laypeople use the term 'divots.' In the *profession*, we call them 'randomized aeration.'" "Interesting," she says. She takes another look at the randomized aeration, nods thoughtfully, and then requests your card. "I'm all out," you reply, "but just visit my website." "What's it called?" she asks. "It's called," you say, "Master of the Lawn."

## 21

Some Master. You have been out here for over an hour and are only two-thirds done. And now it will take much longer because you are headed inside for a beer break.

## 22

Your wife is in the kitchen, so you pause near the fridge and begin telling her about the racist woman who just tried to hire you. Your wife is not in the mood to hear about the racist woman, though, because she is cleaning, her least favorite thing in the world to do. For even longer than you have wanted a John Deere E180 26HP riding lawn mower with a V-twin engine and a beer holder or a Beretta M92 semiautomatic pistol, she has wanted a Merry Maid. You think that's outrageous. No woman should ever hire another woman to clean her own house, in your estimation, unless she is missing a leg. You made the mistake of saying that once but you are determined not to make it now, even after she baits you. "To keep this house clean," she says, "I am really considering becoming an amputee." She stares at you and waits for your response. "Oh, *snap*!" you exclaim, after opening the fridge. "No more beer!" Off to the store you go.

## 23

It has been one of those days, so wouldn't you know it: the moment you place your six-pack on the counter, the cashier asks for your ID. Twenty years ago, when you were in your thirties, long before your hair thinned and grayed and you had reason to take pride in your youthful appearance, this would have been a reasonable and welcomed request. You still look young for your age, but not young enough by a long shot to be carded. You definitely do not look younger than the white cashier doing the carding, or the three white customers who were directly in front of you and not carded. "Jesus Christ," you say, shaking your head. *"Jesus Christ."*

If you decide that Jesus Christ cares about you being carded, consider using a professional therapist instead of your wife, and continue to paragraph 24.

If you decide Jesus Christ does not care that you are being carded, and that some white privilege bullshit directed at you, especially pathetic examples of it like this, *can* be ignored, continue to paragraph 25.

## 24

You refuse to show your ID. The cashier refuses to sell you the beer. You leave it on the counter after offering him some advice, and then head home to stew while finishing your lawn with your puny electric mower, upset enough, you believe, if only you had the means, to shoot someone. Your story ends here.

## 25

You show your ID while chuckling at the pathetic cashier. You chuckle some more while thinking about his pathetic self during your trip home. But once you arrive, you put him out of your mind, for your thoughts have turned to the beer you are placing in your refrigerator, except for one bottle. That one goes in the freezer. It will be brought to chilled perfection in approximately twenty minutes, which gives you just enough time to finish the lawn before receiving that delectable treat, unless, of course, your friendly neighbor with the

MAGA sign comes outside, as he often does when you are mowing, and attempts to strike up a conversation. He probably will not, though. He must know how pissed his sign has made you. Unless he thinks it is not a declaration of his racism and white supremacy and he actually believes he can support Trump solely for his tax breaks and border security. Is that kind of bifurcated thinking even possible? Surely it is not, certainly no more possible than you, say, getting away with stealing his MAGA sign.

If you decide it would be possible to get away with stealing his MAGA sign, go to paragraph 26.

If you decide it would not be possible to get away with stealing his MAGA sign, go to paragraph 27.

## 26

It would not be possible. Your neighbor would discover you during the night creeping across his lawn wearing a ski mask, mistake you for a burglar, and shoot you dead with his Beretta M92 semiautomatic pistol. Your story would end with you face down in his petunias.

## 27

It would be hysterical, though, if you could. One day you might even tell him what you had done, and you'd likely share a good laugh about it, assuming that the Trump fever will break at some point and white people will come to their senses. Perhaps by then white landscapers will do as masterful a job of mowing your lawn as you are now. And when you are outside admiring their work, people driving along Main Street will slow down to yell something at you that is drowned out by the traffic noise but which you can safely assume is complimentary.

If you chose to believe in such a hopeful future, good for you. Your story ends here.

If you would like to believe in such a hopeful future but are having trouble doing so, return to paragraph 17. That is the one, you might recall, about a white child standing alone in the rain, holding a cardboard "Black Lives Matter" sign high over his head. Your story ends there.

# TURNING THE PAGE

There is a popular television show called *Finding Your Roots* in which celebrities' ancestries are traced as far back as possible, sometimes for centuries, before the results are presented by the esteemed Harvard scholar Henry Louis Gates Jr. Gates and a celebrity sit across from each other at a table on which rests a big book containing the research team's efforts, such as birth and death certificates, photos, letters, diaries, newspaper clippings, genetic analysis, and, often, a slave's bill of sale. The show's white guests occasionally discover that this slave was a family member, but this is uncommon. For most Black guests, however, there almost invariably comes the moment when Gates, heretofore lighthearted and jovial, becomes somber, nods at the big book in which the slave ancestor is about to be revealed, and says, "Please turn the page."

Brenda and I like the show for its combination of history, sleuthing, and intrigue, though I do not like it for evoking in me a combination of envy, bitterness, and confusion. Envy at how the lineage of the white guests is unpredictable; bitterness about the slaves to whom the Black guests predictably lead; and confusion when one of these Black guests turns the page and appears shocked to see the name of an eight-year-old boy who was their great-great-great-grandfather purchased for sixty-two dollars and a goat, as if family lore had placed this relative not in the cotton fields of Georgia but the vineyards of France. The first time this happened, I faced Brenda and asked, "Didn't they see that coming?" to which she responded "*Shush!*" And so each subsequent time, there I sat confused while Brenda and the celebrity grew teary-eyed, or openly wept, or, as in the case of the musician Pharrell Williams, became inconsolable.

Williams is best known for his Grammy Award–winning song "Happy." In 2013, it topped the charts in the United States, Ireland, Canada, and two dozen other countries. It has sold over two million copies worldwide, been streamed nearly a million times, and recently was named the most played song of the 2010s. Countless people across the globe posted videos of themselves dancing and singing along to "Happy" as if it were their personal anthem, expressly written for them, and in a way, as Gates noted, it was. "It shows how fundamentally human we are," he said of the song's universal appeal. "How you can speak to the human soul, beyond language, race, ethnicity, if you find the right message." And the right messenger, someone whose own soul, to paraphrase Oprah Winfrey, was the song's direct and necessary origin. Given this context, and with lyrics from "Happy" playing in my head—*Clap along if you feel like a room without a roof / Clap along if you feel like happiness is the truth*—it was gut-wrenching to watch Pharrell, during the course of the show, come undone.

Gates, with his voice full of concern, always asks his guests how the unveiling of their slave ancestry makes them feel. While they *did* see it coming, they often respond, there was something about being presented documents with an actual name, and, in a broader sense, with the actual corrupt values upon which this country was founded, that threw them for a loop. I should not, I know, find their reaction confusing. It makes as much sense as my feeling bitter about the fact of slavery, despite my determination to keep this emotion at bay. Instead of dwelling on the atrocities slaves endured, it is my longstanding practice to focus on the attributes that enabled the slaves' endurance. Fortitude and faith. Courage. Toughness. Hope, an undying hope. And I am in full agreement with Gates's assertion that retrieving their lost stories "can be an act of restoration, not only of our ancestors' resilience, but of the resiliency of the entire human race."

But sometimes, I confess, and with increasing frequency as I age, when the topic of slavery is broached, I am not in the mood to take a positive approach. Nor am I in the mood to be bitter. Rather, I wish simply to be me. As Pharrell became overwhelmed by the distressing contents of the big book that had been prepared for him, it was apparent that he wished the same for himself. "This is messing with my mind," he told Gates. "This is messing with my spirit. This is messing with who I am. It's messing with everything I represent." It was, in short, messing with his happiness.

That was understandable, especially since the finding of his roots was uniquely intense, as one of the documents provided to him contained the literal words of his great-great-great-aunt, a woman named Jane Arrington. Anguish was clearly visible on Pharrell's face as he read aloud this passage of hers: "We lived in log houses with stick and dirt chimneys. They called them the slave houses. I worked on the farm, cutting corn stalks, and tending to cattle. . . . Sometimes I swept the yards after working all day. There was the task of cotton to be picked and spun."

At the time her words were recorded, Ms. Arrington was eighty years old, the first ten of those years having been spent in bondage. Her account would not have been available but for the government-sponsored Slave Narratives from the Federal Writing Project of the 1930s, which conducted 2,300 interviews with former slaves. And few firsthand accounts of being human chattel would reach a vast portion of the American public were it not for a popular show like *Finding Your Roots*. That, in a nutshell, is the show's great value, for it is, above all else, a highly effective teaching tool. And like all highly effective teaching tools, it inspires deep introspection, as appeared to be the instantaneous effect on Pharrell. "What kind of people?" he rhetorically asked Gates, in reference to Ms. Arrington's owners. "What kind of people?" Recognizing that Pharrell had reached his emotional limit, Gates sought to give him time to recover by stopping the tapping of the show.

When the taping resumed weeks later, Gates observed to Pharrell, "To me, it seemed like you were trying not to cry. But what's wrong with crying? We have so much to cry about as a people." Pharrell agreed. Then he explained that crying, for some people—people whose monumental fame, I might add, derives from a song called "Happy"—was a thing best done in private. And with that, he read more of his great-great-great-aunt's narrative and turned the remaining pages of the big book, all while keeping his emotions in check. As the program reached its end, Gates asked one final question: had going through this process changed what he felt about being an American? Without pause, Pharrell strove for positivity, the inclination with which I am so familiar. "I love America," he said, "for its progression. There has been progression for the oppressed. But not enough. And that is what keeps me optimistic. There's untapped potential that we haven't hit. And I still love America."

Gates concluded the show on that uplifting note. And that uplifting note, I decided, was as good as any for me to take a hiatus from watching the show. The next time it aired, I told Brenda I had a ton of papers to grade and left the living room to busy myself next door in my office. As I sat at my desk, however, I could hear Gates's voice, not clearly enough to make out his words, but clearly enough to find them distracting. It was the kind of scenario of which someone with an overactive imagination, such as mine, could make much use, as I did.

A big book . . . two men, one a scholar, the other a slave . . .

And overhead, a wall calendar . . . April 1790 . . .

. . . The scholar opens the big book, signaling the show has begun . . .

There, on the first page, is the slave's name, Nate, followed by a summary of what is known of his life. He was born approximately fifty years prior. His ancestors and their whereabouts are a mystery, including his parents, who are believed to have been sold to a distant plantation when Nate was an infant. He's worked the fields since he could walk. He can neither read nor write, other than his name, but he can cite the Bible, chapter and verse, with his favorite being 2 Corinthians 3:17: "Now the Lord is the Spirit, and where the Spirit of the Lord is, there is Freedom." He is married, though not in the eyes of the State, his union with his wife made in the customary way of jumping a broom and pouring libations. They are expecting a child. Nate knows very little of the world beyond the rows of cotton in which he toils, and of course, he knows nothing of the future collected in the big book. At the scholar's instruction, Nate turns the page.

The beginning is grim. The first documents offer only the cold facts of what the next decade will bring: his death; just two children attributed to him when he knows he has four; auctions of aunts and uncles; lynchings of cousins and brothers; the missing and unaccounted for. Where are all the stories, Nate wonders, that could place kinfolk here and there, or reveal something of their character, their personhood? Such a big book, he thinks, full of rich, complicated lives reduced to the evidence of their bondage, and this, in a nutshell, is the show's great limitation—due not to some fault of the scholar and his researchers, but to the corrupt values of our country's founding. Nate is distressed by much of the book's contents, but soon he grows comforted, for the scholar had found a thread leading from his firstborn to her firstborn, and from that firstborn to others, generation after generation of progeny until the scholar, whose manner to this point has been somber, smiles as he nods at the big book and says, "Turn the page."

Nate does. Before him is a photo of a baby, swaddled in a blanket. Beneath it are three words, someone's name, he surmises, for the middle one he recognizes.

"This," the scholar says, "is your great-great-great-grandson."

Nate replies, "He has my name."

"Yes, he does. And you know what else he has?"

"No, sir."

"The benefit," he says, "of the Negroes' boundless hope."

Nate weeps at this, for he knows it can mean but one thing. He again looks at the child, taking in his features, and taking in, too, the progress the boy represents, the resilience.

"Does it surprise you," the scholar asks, "to discover your descendants are free?"

"Honestly," Nate says, "I saw it coming."

"And how does that make you feel?" asks the scholar. "How does it make you feel knowing what's to come?"

"It makes me feel," Nate says, "happy."

# Acknowledgments

This book was made possible with a grant from the Guggenheim Foundation. I am enormously grateful to my agent, Katherine Flynn of Calligraph Literary Agency, for her tireless advocacy, and to all the good folks at Amistad, especially VP and Editorial Director Abby West, for her sharp eye and excellent advice, and Assistant Editor Makayla Tabron, for skillfully and joyfully guiding me through this process. For their support and assistance, thank you to Bob Atwan, Lundy Braun, Jim Canavan, Donna Gaines, Mary Grant, Shaylin Hogan, Maria Kingdon, Tom Kingdon, Maria Koundoura, Lee Pelton, Marc Rando, Stephanie Rando, Jan Roberts-Breslin, Tracy Sherrod, Johnny Skoyles, and John Trimbur. Lastly, thank you to Brenda Molife, my best friend and best critic, and to our sons, Adrian and Dorian, my best gift.

A version of "Minstrel I" originally appeared in the *Chicago Quarterly Review* as "An American Right." "It's Hard Out Here for a Memoirist" originally appeared in *Prairie Schooner* and was reprinted in *The Best American Essays 2024*.

# About the Author

Jerald Walker is the author of *How to Make a Slave and Other Essays*, which was a finalist for the National Book Award and winner of the Massachusetts Book Award; *The World in Flames: A Black Boyhood in a White Supremacist Doomsday Cult*; and *Street Shadows: A Memoir of Race, Rebellion, and Redemption*, which received the PEN/New England Award for Nonfiction. His work has appeared in publications such as the *Harvard Review, Creative Nonfiction*, the *Iowa Review*, the *New York Times*, the *Washington Post,* and *Mother Jones,* as well as six editions of the Best American Essays series and in the Pushcart Prizes. A recipient of fellowships from the Guggenheim Foundation, the National Endowment for the Arts, and the James A. Michener Foundation, Walker is a professor of Creative Writing and African American Literature at Emerson College. He lives outside Boston, Massachusetts.